ADVANCE PRAISE

"Yes!!! A resource for teachers that actually defines the standards, builds knowledge, and provides scaffolds and supports for *both* teachers and students! This easy-to-read book contains over 100 materials ready for immediate implementation. Explanations and models (with annotations) tied to authentic literature are provided. It's the perfect addition to any CCSS-aligned curriculum or program. Teaching constructed response has never been easier!"

—Dena Mortensen, Supervisor of Elementary Reading and
Language Arts, Waterbury Public Schools, CT

"Nancy Boyles's book is appropriately titled: it's an awesome guide to teaching students how to read closely and construct an answer to every type of comprehension question. The skills students develop with Boyles's methods will serve them well on standardized tests and beyond, as they will read and write more carefully and think more clearly. A blessing for busy teachers, Boyles's book offers detailed lesson plans and abundant sample questions on prose and poetry selections."

—Geraldine Woods, teacher and author of *25 Great Sentences and How They Got That Way* and *Sentence. A Period-to-Period Guide to Building Better Readers and Writers*

"Nancy Boyles's newest book holds the secret formula teachers have been looking for to strategically teach the components of a well-written constructed response. *Writing Awesome Answers to Comprehension Questions* takes the process and breaks it down into clear, easy-to-follow steps. The text is loaded with instructional strategies and resources for immediate use, including Anchor Charts, Checklists, and Answer Frames."

—Michelle Dupuis, Academic Coach, Natchaug School, Willimantic, CT

"At construction sites, they put windows in the walls so you can see inside the building site. Nancy Boyles gives you such a window into how students can build meaningful 'constructed' responses. More importantly, she delivers thoughtful, practical tools teachers can use to help students read carefully and respond accurately. These tools include anchor charts, cue cards, and ways to have students engage with various media types. As usual, a can't-miss text."

—Dr. Michael J. Rafferty, Director of Teaching and Learning, Derby Public Schools, Derby, CT, and author of *30 Big Ideas Lessons in Small Groups*

"The wait is over. *Writing Awesome Answers to Comprehension Questions* is absolutely brilliant. Nancy Boyles has bestowed a toolbox upon teachers, with which to get students writing about reading. Teachers will discover numerous mini lessons, instructional strategies, texts aligned to questions, anchor charts, rubrics, checklists, and more. This systematic approach to analytical reading instruction is a complete guide to supporting students of all reading levels to read for meaning and answer questions deeply."

—Christina O'Brien, Assistant Principal/Special Education Supervisor, Naubuc Elementary School, Glastonbury, CT

WRITING AWESOME ANSWERS to COMPREHENSION QUESTIONS

(even the hard ones)

Norton Books in Education

WRITING AWESOME ANSWERS to COMPREHENSION QUESTIONS

(even the hard ones)

NANCY BOYLES

W. W. NORTON & COMPANY

Independent Publishers Since 1923

Note to Readers: Models and/or techniques described in this volume are illustrative or are included for general informational purposes only; neither the publisher nor the author(s) can guarantee the efficacy or appropriateness of any particular recommendation in every circumstance. As of press time, the URLs displayed in this book link or refer to existing sites. The publisher and author are not responsible for any content that appears on third-party websites.

For information about permission to reproduce selections from this book, write to Permissions, W. W. Norton & Company, Inc., 500 Fifth Avenue, New York, NY 10110

For information about special discounts for bulk purchases, please contact W. W. Norton Special Sales at specialsales@wwnorton.com or 800-233-4830

Manufacturing by Sheridan Books
Design by Joe Lops
Production manager: Katelyn MacKenzie

Library of Congress Cataloging-in-Publication Data

Names: Boyles, Nancy N., 1948– author.
Title: Writing awesome answers to comprehension questions (even the hard ones) /
    Nancy Boyles.
Description: First edition. | New York : W. W. Norton & Company, [2021] | Series:
    Norton books in education | Includes bibliographical references and index.
Identifiers: LCCN 2020029802 | ISBN 9781324015918 (paperback) |
    ISBN 9781324015925 (epub)
Subjects: LCSH: English language—Composition and exercises—Study and
    teaching. | Reading comprehension—Study and teaching. | Reading
    comprehension—Problems, exercises, etc.
Classification: LCC LB1576 .B556 2021 | DDC 372.47—dc23
LC record available at https://lccn.loc.gov/2020029802

W. W. Norton & Company, Inc., 500 Fifth Avenue, New York, N.Y. 10110
www.wwnorton.com

W. W. Norton & Company Ltd., 15 Carlisle Street, London W1D 3BS

1 2 3 4 5 6 7 8 9 0

With thanks to Josh and Andrea, who have stolen my heart, and whose hard work with early reading has demonstrated to me one more time that a solid foundation in word skills is a necessary prerequisite for one day writing awesome answers to comprehension questions. And with thanks as well to these same special friends for reminding me of the importance of children seeing themselves as readers. Their trust in us, their teachers, to empower them as literacy learners is immeasurable. May we never betray that trust.

Nancy Boyles
January 2021

CONTENTS

INTRODUCTION

Focusing Our Writing Lens on Comprehension

The world of writing is a wide one. This book explores only a narrow piece of that world: analytical writing that requires short answers—specifically answers to standards-based comprehension questions. We call these *constructed responses* because students are tasked with constructing the answers themselves, as opposed to choosing from a list of options.

There are many issues to address around constructed response to maximize the power of teachers' instruction and the potential of students' learning. In Part I of this book we'll unpack those issues, identifying best instructional practices. Parts II and III turn those practices into ready-to-use tools designed to lead students to success as analytical readers and writers.

But before delving into the strategies that are effective for teaching constructed response, let's take a moment to trace the history and meaning of the term itself.

What IS Constructed Response? A Trip Down Terminology Lane

The term *constructed response* gained popularity with the arrival of the Common Core, separating questions of this type from *selected response*—also a relative newcomer to the language of literacy instruction and assessment. For selected response, think *multiple choice*. Following the question are several possible answers, typically A, B, C, D. In the past, students would "select" just one of those options, though now students may be instructed to choose any number of options, or "all that apply."

Constructed response questions are different in that students must "construct" or write the answer themselves. In the past, a more commonly used term was *open-ended question* because students could respond in more than one way and still be correct—as long as they could justify their response with textual evidence. These were sometimes called *short answer questions* because the intended length was shorter than a full essay, although technically, a constructed response could be any length.

What we used to regard as the *essay*, in particular the infamous *Five Paragraph Essay*, has been repackaged as a *performance-based task* (in some cases, simply called a *performance task*). Or it might be labeled an *extended response*. There is no longer a prescribed number of paragraphs. I've also heard the term *long-writes* for any lengthy writing task, and *short-writes* for shorter pieces.

One of the key distinctions between writing genres was that students wrote *stories* (narrative writing), or they wrote reports, essays, research papers, and the like, which were considered *analytical writing*. But even these lines have become blurred. On some state testing sites I've noted references to *narrative essays*, which on closer examination are tasks where students are asked to write *stories*. Are you confused yet? Think how confusing all of this must be to students.

For the purposes of this book, let's use this working definition for constructed response:

Constructed Responses are analytical writing tasks, typically shorter than a full-length essay, where students respond to comprehension questions related to one or more literary or informational texts.

What's in This Book (and What's Not), and How It Will Help You and Your Students

Like so many difficulties that students face in school, the problem we see on the surface may represent the symptom more than the underlying cause. This is often true with constructed response—the real issue may be more about reading than writing. Sometimes the reading problem relates to decoding. We have some students who can't answer comprehension questions because they can't figure out the words in what they read—either the text or the question about the text. You will not find the solution to that issue (lack of foundational reading skills) in this book, although it certainly needs to be resolved. However, we also have many students who *can* read the words, but still don't comprehend. Those are the readers we aim to impact here.

Part I: Writing Awesome Answers, Unpacked explains the thinking behind the hands-on resources provided to students. This part begins with what a lesson might look like with actual kids, followed by an examination of what it means to teach—not just test—comprehension and the kinds of questions that encourage deep thinking.

- **Chapter 1: Constructed Response in Action: A Virtual Classroom Visit**
  Observe from afar a group of third graders and a teacher (me) engaged in a small group lesson that connects analytical reading and writing through constructed response.

- **Chapter 2: The Road to Awesome Answers: Teaching (Not Just Testing) Comprehension**

  What do we mean by *teaching* students how to respond to comprehension questions, and why is this instruction so important? Then, how we can turn today's student outcomes into tomorrow's learning goals by reflecting on students' performance? Find answers here.

- **Chapter 3: Good Questions: 41 Ways into a Text, Indexed to Concepts and Teaching Tools**

  Questioning has changed based on new standards and new expectations for rigor, with the good news that there are now many more lenses through which we can help students appreciate a text. Learn what's new with questioning strategies here. At the end of this chapter, find a guide to the best tools—anchor charts and checklists—perfectly aligned to any question you teach.

Part II: Hands-on Support for Reading and Understanding provides ready-to-use resources for analytical reading, for students whose difficulty with constructed response begins with difficulty comprehending. Awesome answers begin with awesome teaching, so we'll begin with what comprises each minilesson and end with the tools that bring these lessons to life.

- **Chapter 4: Minilessons for Analytical Reading**

  First, you will find an explanation of the comprehension concept. The concept is described in language that intermediate students will understand, and can be read to or with them. Also noted in the minilesson are suggestions for choosing texts aligned to the question you wish to teach, as well as titles of the anchor charts and checklists matched to each question for student practice.

- **Chapter 5: Tools for Analytical Reading**

  The 41 anchor charts and checklists guide students as they read more closely to analyze concepts like author's craft, connections between texts, and character traits. These charts and checklists are interactive to provide hands-on practice.

Part III: Hands-on Support for Responding and Writing moves beyond support in reading to strategies for helping students respond in writing. For some students, support in reading comprehension is all they will need to write quality answers to constructed response questions. But other students need direct support with the writing itself. Support can take many forms, and truth to tell, should include oral as well as written response. Note that the resources in Part III can be photocopied from the book, or downloaded and printed from the provided URL, for distribution to students.

- **Chapter 6: Cue Cards for Oral Rehearsal**

  Rehearsing a response out loud before committing it to paper is a critical (and often missing) step for many students. Cue cards provided in this section for the rehearsal of every question are a wonderful tool for individual or paired practice.

- **Chapter 7: Sample Constructed Responses**

  Helping students analyze responses to comprehension questions is an extra layer of support for visual learners, as well as those students for whom another mode of practice would be beneficial. Two sample responses for each question are included to share and discuss. There is one answer that would receive a full score, and a second one that would earn a partial score based on inaccuracies or omissions. A scoring analysis is included at the end of this chapter for the response with a partial score. A reference to the text used for the models is provided in case you wish to access it for your own class to read before analyzing the response.

- **Chapter 8: Answer Frames for Constructed Response**

  This is the final scaffold and is intended for students who need even more support: sentence-starters with lines provided to organize their response.

- **Appendix: Study Guide with Suggested Resources: Teaching Practices That Lead to Awesome Answers**

  Here's a quick review of 10 key points for teachers to contemplate as they strive to improve students' reading comprehension and written response—by fine-tuning their own instructional practices. Use students' needs as an opportunity to continue to grow professionally.

  When we think of constructed response, we think first of how we can help students *write* better. But remember that students are writing about their *reading*. For the best answers, students will initially need to unlock the deep meaning the text holds, then craft a response that reflects their capacity to put their thinking into words. This is the teaching that will rescue readers from writing answers that are just okay to writing answers that are, well . . . awesome.

WRITING AWESOME ANSWERS to COMPREHENSION QUESTIONS

(even the hard ones)

Santo Domingo, the capital

...her life and my dad said in Spanish "careful

...ing right?" she asked back. I was laughing really hard because that

...een. The good thing is that no harsh feelings get caught in the action.

...the best for me, they want me to go to school and graduate with a

...degree studying. A regular hourly phone they repeat to me is

...the monetary problems to us" something I can never contradict.

...hair styling 6 days a week. She studied that on one of the best

...the Dominican Republic at the time which was around 20 years

...It's a good thing. My dad is a sales man for a type company

...focus on high-quality windows that are tough enough to

...on the ocean areas which are the most touristic based

...I want, what I dream of, and no matter how big or

...to them and to never let go because dreams are

...d our dreams can become true makes us

...hange, our dreams change too. My dad and I

...rew up. I was 14 at the time. He simply

...He looked at me and said "Fidel, I know,

...him the you-think-I'm-stupid look

...I said. He took a deep breath and

...to achieve

...s well on tests.

...m, I applaud him

...ports, and a social life. He

...at he had gotten accepted to almost

...our class with a 4.2 GPA? On the night

...students received scholarships for the

...ip he got was for $500. The night

...he wasn't going to get any more

...Then, the final name was ca...

...figures. I

...hen he w

PART I

Writing Awesome Answers, Unpacked

CHAPTER I
CONSTRUCTED RESPONSE IN ACTION:
A Virtual Classroom Visit

Six third-graders filed into their school's media center. There were smiles all around, but also a few quizzical looks as they noted the dozen or so teachers assembled near the table where we were planning to do our lesson. The teachers and I had spent the past hour of our professional development session discussing the challenges of writing quality answers to reading comprehension questions. Now I was ready to teach a lesson where I'd demonstrate strategies aimed at making constructed response (the current terminology more manageable, even to younger students, and those who might otherwise struggle with connecting analytical reading and writing.

When I model a lesson, I ask teachers to send me students who are *not* the best readers and writers in the class. While a group of superstars would be likely to do well with whatever concept I introduce (and make me look good!), teachers would be quick to point out that "of course, *those* kids could handle whatever the new learning entailed . . . but what about the *other* kids?" I also enjoy working with younger students to show that rigor can indeed be developmentally appropriate, despite the grade level.

On this morning, I had a group of students with mixed abilities, among them, a child on the autism spectrum, two English learners, and a little boy with ADHD. There were still a few wary glances at all those teachers in the room: "Don't worry about them," I reassured. "They're here mostly to watch *me*." And so we began.

"Usually when I come to a school to teach a lesson, I teach about reading or writing. Today we're working on both. First, we'll read two short stories, then answer a question in writing where we connect the two texts." I placed the question written in large font on the table where everyone could see it and read it aloud.

> What is the central idea in the fables, "The Ant and the Dove" and "The Lion and the Mouse"? Compare how the author developed this central idea.

Deconstruct the Question

I've learned over the years that spending some time deconstructing the question before the reading is like money in the bank when students move from reading to writing. "What are the most important words in this question?" I asked now.

"Central idea. What's that?" one student responded. No one seemed to have heard that term before, so we clarified.

"Have you ever heard the term *theme* or *lesson* or *moral*?" They had. "All of these terms mean about the same thing. You'll probably see central idea a lot on your big state test." (Because it's the language used in the Common Core—though I didn't add this point to our conversation.)

Students also identified *compare*, with which they were familiar. No one mentioned *develop*, but I paused to discuss it because its relevance to standards-based assessments is more significant than you might expect. "When the question asks how the author *develops* something, how does that matter to the evidence you include?" I helped them understand that *develop* means you need to show how something grows and changes from the beginning to the end of the text, kind of like a summary. You need to include details from the beginning, middle, and end of a text. "This is different from the way you may have answered comprehension questions in the past where you chose a couple of details and that was enough. This will make your answers longer."

This was a quick conversation because I needed to get to the reading itself. I don't like to model small group lessons that last longer than 20 minutes, because I know classroom teachers face time constraints that limit them to about 20 minutes, too. In this case, I warned everyone in advance that this would be a 30–40 minute session since I was combining multiple lessons; I wouldn't be back the next day to complete the sequence of steps.

"We're going to read two short fables," I began. "What's a fable?" Even third graders are experienced with this genre and easily told me they are short stories with animals who talk, and there's a moral at the end. Good job! I distributed our two texts, "The Ant and the Dove" and "The Lion and the Mouse." These were both retrieved from Project Gutenberg, an archive of out-of-copyright sources free for any use. Both tales are included at the end of this chapter so my lesson can be replicated if you choose to do so.

In truth, these are easy-to-read texts, just right for third-graders, although I've also used them with fourth, fifth, and even sixth-graders. Of course, students will read grade-level passages on state assessments, and for classroom reading instruction as well. But when your focus is constructed response—in this case, the art of comparing central ideas—consider simple stories or informational pieces so the complexity of the reading won't get in the way of the writing process you're trying to teach.

Identify the Central Idea

Also, for ease of access, I applied a strategy I use sparingly: choral reading. Reading the fables out loud together assured we'd complete the reading efficiently, without waiting for slow finishers. First, we read "The Ant and the Dove." "Who can tell me what happened in the first part of this story?" I asked. A couple of volunteers offered that Ant was about to drown, but Dove tossed him a leaf so he could float safely to the bank of the river. Another student contributed that in the second part of the story, a hunter was about to trap Dove, so Ant stung him on the foot which made the hunter yelp in pain, which made Dove fly away. "Oh, I get it," Shira announced. "It's like if you're nice to someone, they'll be nice back to you." Well done, Shira, except this time I wasn't looking for an instant insight.

I next planned to share a strategy for helping to identify the central idea. How would this be received if students had already identified the concept? We would see. I pulled out an anchor chart I'd created (see Anchor Chart 4: Topics and Central Ideas for Narrative Fiction and Nonfiction). "In the first column," I began, "these are *topics*." I pointed to a few examples: Friendship, Honesty, Persistence. But a central idea is something *about* a topic—like *Be honest, even when it's difficult* or *How you tell the truth makes a difference to people's feelings*." Then I asked students to consider the list with me.

"Let's look at the topics first and decide which one is the best match for our story. Then we can look across the page at the next column and figure out the actual central idea." As I read through the list of topics, there was modest support for a few of them. "Okay," I suggested, "keep looking, and at the end we'll decide which one is the *very* best." When we reached Kindness on the list, there was a loud chorus of "That's the one." Of the three central idea options, everyone agreed that *If you are kind to someone, they may be kind to you in return* was a perfect match.

About 20 minutes had already ticked by. This would have signaled the end of today's work if this was my own class, and I had the luxury of returning to the lesson the following day. But now I needed to soldier on. "The Lion and the Mouse" was a quick read (also read chorally) because students were already familiar with this story:

Mouse is looking for food and stumbles upon a sleeping Lion. The Lion wakes and threatens to eat the mouse. But the mouse begs to be let go, promising to help the lion someday. The lion thinks this is unlikely but does release the mouse. Then one day the lion is caught in a hunter's snare and the little mouse chews through the ropes to set the lion free. Again, kindness was repaid.

Discuss the Task: Compare and Contrast

"Are these stories *exactly* alike?" I asked.

"Well," reasoned Miguel, "in 'The Ant and the Dove,' the characters were nice to each other from the beginning. But in 'The Lion and the Mouse,' the lion was rude at first." I might have chosen a stronger word than "rude" for a character who was intent on eating another character. But the rest of the group nodded approvingly, so we continued. I explained that it's always good to note a major difference in two texts when comparing them, so this contrast would be a good one to mention when writing an answer to the comprehension question we identified earlier.

We had read our texts, discussed them, identified the common theme, and noted a significant difference between the stories, a strategy to keep in mind when writing a response. So, were students now ready to begin writing? I didn't think so.

Rehearse Answers Orally

Students often participate enthusiastically in a discussion about a text, wowing you with seemingly perfect understanding of what they read. But then they return to their seat minutes later to put that same answer on paper and whine, "I have no idea what to write." What's missing from this equation that would get kids to pick up their pencil with conviction and plunge in? What's missing now, and has been missing for a very long time, is what I call oral rehearsal: saying something exactly as you intend to write it.

1. The [central idea] of both stories is _____.

2. Something important about the similarity and difference between these stories is _____.

3. In [Source #1], the author showed this central idea with these events: _____

   _____.

4. In [Source #2], the author showed this central idea with these events: _____

   _____.

5. This [central idea] is important because _____.

For this answer, I distributed a card to students that included five sentence stems. This supported students in two ways. First, it provided a logical sequence of steps so they could see how their answer would flow. It also offered guidance for how to begin their sentences, which seems to be students' biggest hang-up, and why they're reluctant to risk writing that first word.

We read the sentences one at a time and I asked individual students to complete the sentence(s) for me. Sentences 1 and 2 were easy, but 3 and 4 were more involved. "Remember," I cautioned, "you need to show how each author *developed* the central idea, a little summary of the events at the beginning, middle, and end of the story." For now, we wouldn't respond to Sentence 5.

Finally, Write!

Next, I divided students into pairs and modeled how this would look, choosing one student to be my partner. When it was the students' turn, I listened in as they spoke their answers, prompting as needed. Mostly, though, I offered praise: "I love how you're looking back at the stories to make sure you have all the right details." Going back to the text is a perpetual battle, but one worth winning.

"Now that we've *said* our answer, do you think it would be easier to *write* it?" I asked when oral rehearsal buzz ceased. It would be a "piece of cake," they thought. I handed each student an answer frame (page 303) and began explaining the directions, though I didn't get far. "We know how to do this," they assured me. At that point, my role was to get out of their way.

They wrote. And wrote. And wrote. There were a few complaints of hands that hurt and sighs from needing to do "all this writing." But I was in full cheerleader mode: "You know, I've noticed that if your hand hurts, that probably means you've got enough details." They kept writing, pleased with themselves about their obvious success.

"One last thing," I said as our session neared its end. "We never talked about Sentence 5 on your Cue Card: *This [central lesson] is important because* _____. The tricky thing about Sentence 5 is that the question doesn't ask you to mention this. But good writers (who want to score well on important assessments) extend their answer a little by including not just the evidence, but why it's important."

There can be lots of reasons why the lesson is important, and many ways to explain it, but we were all maxed out on new learning today, so I chose one option to share: a personal connection. "Do you think the lesson we talked about today (kindness toward others) is important only to characters in a fable, or to us, too?" Of course they thought this was also a "real people lesson," and I gave an example: "When I was your age, if I offered to help my mom clean up after dinner, she was kind to me and let me stay up a few minutes beyond my regular bedtime. I think that's just like the characters in these fables who showed kindness to each other." Students quickly shared their own examples and completed the last part of their frame.

Reflection

"It's a wrap," I told them. "Great job! Why do you think you did so well answering this question?" "The chart with the central ideas," someone replied. "But mostly the card for saying the answer out loud," someone else added.

"I think both of those helped," I acknowledged. "But remember, you won't always have that card, or the answer frame. You'll need to think about what makes sense when you're comparing texts: First, state the central idea. Next, say one big thing about how the stories are the same or different. Then, summarize what happens in each story to show the central idea. Finally, tell why the central idea is important." We reviewed this sequence a few times until everyone mostly had it. They could come back to that tomorrow for more reinforcement.

As the children left the media center and teachers reassembled for the lesson debrief, one teacher pulled me aside: "That seemed almost *too* easy. What's the catch?" No catch, I hope, no smoke and mirrors. If students found it easy, I hope that was because many components of good instruction came together in just the right way. With this lesson as a backdrop, let's identify those components and deconstruct them.

Sources Used for the Virtual Lesson

THE ANT AND THE DOVE

An Ant, walking by the river one day, said to himself, "How nice and cool this water looks! I must drink some of it." But as he began to drink, his foot slipped, and he fell in.

"Oh, somebody please help me, or I shall drown!" cried he.

A Dove, sitting in a tree that overhung the river, heard him, and threw him a leaf. "Climb up on that leaf," said she, "and you will float ashore."

The Ant climbed up onto the leaf, which the wind blew to the shore, and he stepped upon dry land again.

"Good-by, kind Dove," said he, as he ran home. "You have saved my life, and I wish I could do something for you."

"Good-by," said the Dove; "be careful not to fall in again."

A few days after this, when the Dove was busy building her nest, the Ant saw a man just raising his gun to shoot her.

He ran quickly, and bit the man's leg so hard that he cried "Oh! oh!" and dropped his gun.

This startled the Dove, and she flew away. The man picked up his gun, and walked on. When he was gone, the Dove came back to her nest.

"Thank you, my little friend," she said. "You have saved my life."

And the little Ant was overjoyed to think he had been able to do for the Dove what the Dove had so lately done for him.

Retrieved from Project Gutenberg:
https://www.gutenberg.org/files/49010/49010-h/49010-h.htm#Page_26

THE LION AND THE MOUSE

It once happened that a hungry Lion woke to find a Mouse just under his paw. He caught the tiny creature, and was about to make a mouthful of him, when the little fellow looked up, and began to beg for his life.

In most piteous tones the Mouse said: "Do not eat me. I meant no harm coming so near you. If you would only spare my life now, O Lion, I would be sure to repay you!"

The Lion laughed scornfully at this, but it amused him so much that he lifted his paw and let his brave little prisoner go free.

It befell the great Lion, not long afterward, to be in as evil a case as had been the helpless Mouse. And it came about that his life was to be saved by the keeping of the promise he had ridiculed.

He was caught by some hunters, who bound him with a strong rope, while they went away to find means for killing him.

Hearing his loud groans, the Mouse came promptly to his rescue, and gnawed the great rope till the royal captive could set himself free.

"You laughed," the little Mouse said, "at the idea of my being able to be of service to you. You little thought I should repay you. But you see it has come to pass that you are as grateful to me as I was once to you. The weak have their place in the world as truly as the strong."

Retrieved from:
https://www.gutenberg.org/files/49010/49010-h/49010-h.htm#Page_61

CHAPTER 2

THE ROAD TO AWESOME ANSWERS:

TEACHING (NOT JUST TESTING) COMPREHENSION

The alternative to *teaching* comprehension is to simply ask questions and hold students accountable for the answers they produce. If they don't get it right the first time, ask the question again . . . and again . . . and again. This approach assumes that eventually students will catch on. However, what we often see instead is that practice makes *permanent,* not *perfect,* with the same faulty patterns of response showing up in subsequent answers, too. Moreover, when you just ask the question without the benefit of instruction (no matter how many times you ask it), I'd say that's *testing* comprehension, not *teaching* it.

Nonetheless, it's common practice, and advocates of this approach wonder what all the fuss is about. After all, these are *short* answers. How hard can it be to write a few pithy sentences? Turns out, pretty hard. The road to an awesome answer is a bumpy one with potholes to dodge and uncertainty about which way to turn when the fog rolls in. But we can do this. We can first recognize the constructed response challenges that await our students, and next offer the guidance and strategies students need to thrive.

The first challenge is that teaching constructed response begins long before expecting students to write an answer to a question. It is true that for some students the problem is the inability to organize and present their thoughts in writing. But there are many other students who don't write good answers because they didn't understand the reading. Failing to address reading before writing means that a good answer will remain forever beyond the reach of students who need the most help. These students need to understand how to find not only meaning, but *deep* meaning, in a text. They need a lesson (or maybe 41 lessons) in analytical reading.

Analytical Reading Is Systematic Reading

To analyze something implies approaching it systematically. There's a logic to the progression of steps that help you reach your goal—in this case, comprehension. We know how to make instruction systematic: apply the gradual release model. This model begins with lots of teacher support and moves steadily toward student independence. But like anything else in education, we need to implement this model well to achieve the greatest impact. A few guidelines may help.

LINK NEW LEARNING TO KNOWN CONCEPTS

Building comprehension is tricky because there's no standard progression of concepts (or questions). However, be sure that your instruction makes sense. For example, before asking students to compare themes in two texts, make sure they know what "theme" is and can identify it in a single text. Before addressing nuances of characterization like motivation and attitude, build basic concepts like traits and feelings. Once you've established these foundational concepts, then move on to more complex questions that are so important to students' deeper thinking.

EXPLAIN WELL

A good explanation is more than giving directions about how to complete an assignment. What comprehension concept are you teaching? It's the concept that you need to explain, not just the language of the question. Stay focused. Be clear. Remember that the best explanations inform students not only about *what* to do, but *how* to do it. Are you explaining how to recognize text structures? Unpack the process for students by showing how *you* do it.

MODEL BRIEFLY

Keep it short. And keep kids engaged. While you may find your sage words mesmerizing and indispensable, students lose interest quickly when they are not involved. Find small ways to include them in this part of the lesson. Modeling one example is probably enough. Then it's their turn. Think: monitoring. You need to examine their progress so far to know whether you can move on or need to reteach.

PRACTICE, PRACTICE, PRACTICE

One of the most deceptive things about comprehension is that we think we've "taught" a concept, when really, we've just gotten started. Building a comprehension concept is never a one-and-done experience. Introduce it today. Reinforce it tomorrow. And the next day. And the day after that. Keep your eye on the goal: What can students do more independently today than they did yesterday? (Which might be one of the most important questions you ask yourself as a teacher.)

RECOGNIZE THAT INDEPENDENCE IS A MOVING TARGET

No one is disputing the importance of getting students to a point in the learning process where they can apply a comprehension concept without a teacher at close range for emergency support. But independence with a concept today may not yield the same happy results tomorrow. There are many variables. Maybe the new text is more complex, more difficult to understand. Maybe the question is stated in a manner that is less clear. Maybe students have more or less prior knowledge about the topic. While we can't guarantee independence, we can teach in a way that maximizes students' capacity to achieve that goal.

Indeed, the gradual release model applied to reading comprehension can position students to succeed with constructed response. But even when students comprehend well, constructed response needs carefully orchestrated strategies to produce the desired results. One strategy teachers often use to support students' analytical writing is R.A.C.E. But before you "race" to implement this in *your* classroom, understand the possible pitfalls.

R.A.C.E. to Write Great Answers: Not as Easy as It Sounds

R.A.C.E. is an acronym where each letter stands for a component of a quality constructed response. Exactly where it came from is unclear, and there are a few variations. But the basic components are:

Restate the question

Answer the question

Cite evidence to support your answer

Explain the importance

More than just an acronym, teachers regard R.A.C.E. as a formula to guide students as they write their response. But like most formulas, relying on it too much masks the complexities of using it well. What's easy about each of the R.A.C.E. components? What's hard? Students often have a different take on this than their teachers.

Students are quick to reply: "C is hardest" (citing the evidence). This tells me "C" likely gets the most focus in their classroom, although teachers recognize that *all* R.A.C.E. steps can be daunting. Here's how teachers appraise the challenges:

R: <u>RESTATE THE QUESTION</u>

- Sometimes students think that all they need to do to "restate" is to begin their answer with words from the question. While that is one part of meeting the criteria, it is not enough.
- Students who do best with restating understand that they need to recognize the key words in the question and explain, in their own words, what the question is asking them to do. This is especially difficult for English learners and other students who struggle with vocabulary and language issues.
- Sometimes there isn't a question, there's a statement. For example: "This character was motivated by money. Explain how the author shows this throughout the story." Can we find a better word than "question" to define writing tasks?
- Students have never seen questions like some of the ones they're seeing now. They have no idea where to begin.

A: <u>ANSWER THE QUESTION</u>

- This usually requires an inference. If students make an inference that is inaccurate, the rest of their answer will be wrong because they can't follow an incorrect inference with relevant supporting evidence. We underestimate how important this part of a response is. We need to teach inferring more thoroughly.
- The "answer" to the question should be a brief statement: "The main idea is that not all sharks are dangerous." "The craft that the author used in this paragraph is dialogue." Done! Students should leave details out of their basic answer to the question, although they often charge ahead with details that belong under the citation of evidence.

C: <u>CITE EVIDENCE</u>

- The evidence needs to be specific, and some students just focus on generalities: "The character worked hard" instead of "The character worked in a salt mine all day, then came home and did homework for his night classes." They need to *show* instead of *tell*.

- Sometimes students cite evidence by writing lengthy quotes from the text without knowing exactly what the quote means. Quotes can be good evidence, but sometimes students don't know where to stop: "It must be in here somewhere," they reason.

- Sometimes the evidence seems so obvious to students that they don't think they need to write it down. If it's in their head, it must be in the person's head who's reading their answer, too. Students need to understand that you cannot make any assumptions about readers' knowledge when you're writing an answer.

- Sometimes there are multiple parts to a question, but students only cite evidence for one of the parts. For example, if the question is: "What three reasons does the author give for climate change? How does each one affect our climate?" Don't forget about that second part!

- Writing all the necessary evidence requires stamina. Sometimes students run out of energy before they run out of details that should be included in their response.

E: <u>EXPLAIN THE IMPORTANCE</u>

- Sometimes students run out of time before they get to this part.
- Sometimes they don't connect the explanation back to the text so you can't see how the explanation relates to what they read.
- Often students have no idea what to write for this, and just omit it.

Let's imagine that we've navigated all of the complexities of the gradual release model to develop analytical readers and implemented the R.A.C.E. strategy expertly to build understanding of the response process. What should a good answer look like?

Hitting the Target:
High Quality Answers

In our definition of constructed response in the Introduction, we indicated that these are *short* answers. But how short is short? In days gone by, *short* meant quite short, two or three sentences or a brief paragraph. There will still be occasions when the answer is this concise—for example, when students are asked to paraphrase a sentence or two from a source. But now, short answers are more often a chunky paragraph, one-third to one-half a handwritten page. Some assessment guidelines suggest

100–150 words or a character count of perhaps 4,000 characters. (We're not used to thinking in terms of characters on a page and this is confusing to both teachers and students.) A reasonable amount of time to write a short constructed response is about five to seven minutes for students comfortable with the process. Check your state guidelines for specifics, but what is most critical to understand is *why* these answers are now expected to be longer.

Answers are longer because of both the nature of the question and the expected rigor of the response. Many constructed response questions now tap Depth of Knowledge 3, where students must think inferentially and where they will need to defend their answer with substantial textual evidence, as well as well-reasoned insights. For example:

What do you think was the author's purpose for including the text box on page 6?

Contrast this to a question that may have been asked about the same text box in the past:

What information does the author include in the text box on page 6?

The second question requires only basic comprehension where everything a student needs in order to answer is right on the page. If students can accurately describe the author's information, that gets the job done. The first question probes more deeply, seeking abstract thinking and insight. The evidence comes from the text, but the answer comes from the interpretation of the evidence. It's less about being "correct," and more about being a perceptive thinker.

Most (but not all) comprehension questions today lead to longer answers because citing the evidence is just the beginning—or more accurately, the middle. As R.A.C.E. reminds us, first comes the inference; then the evidence to support the inference; and then a little tidbit that too often flies beneath the radar, an explanation of the importance of the evidence: its significance. Most questions don't specifically ask for this extension; students are supposed to just know to include it. Otherwise, they risk receiving less than full credit for the answer they've worked so diligently to craft.

We've done our best to teach students to read well and to write well. Is that the end of our journey? Not quite. Now we need to take a close look at the answers students have written. What can we learn from these answers? How can they inform our next instructional steps?

Generating Actionable Data
That Informs Instruction

During a recent school visit, I was sitting with the literacy coach and principal, giving feedback about the classroom observations we'd just completed. At the end of the chat, the principal thanked me: "This is all good information," he said, "and better yet, it's actionable."

What do we mean by "actionable"? I understand this most simply to mean we can use the information (data) we collect to plan what we will teach next. We can collect the information we need from students' answers using a rubric for teachers and a checklist for students. These tools provide criteria to look for in students' written answers. Most of these criteria are factors we identified in our description of R.A.C.E: the answer itself (often an inference), the evidence to support the answer, and the explanation of importance. This will cover the territory most of the time, but the measurement tool should also be able to accommodate unique features of responses that call for additional components (hence, a couple of boxes for teachers to add their own criteria).

I also think it's helpful to look at students' written language and organizational skills in their response. Although most state assessments only evaluate language competence in longer written pieces like essays, we send the wrong message to kids if we let them think they only need to concern themselves with the *content* of their writing, that *how* they express their thinking in a constructed response doesn't matter.

Beyond the assessment criteria in a rubric, there's the scale that measures the criteria. As with most rubrics, it's not too hard to assign a performance level to the categories designating the best and the worst performance. The top of the scale indicates everything we hope to see in a student product. At the lowest level, the opposite is true: Nothing we wish to see is evident. It's those gray areas in the middle that challenge us. I try to stay away from qualifiers for frequency like *usually, most of the time, sometimes, seldom*—which seem so subjective they're almost useless. For constructed response, I examine the quality: *How* accurate is the answer? *How* spot-on is the evidence and how thoroughly is it developed? *How* insightful is the explanation of importance? And yes, we look at *how* coherent and skilled the writing is, too.

There's one other critical difference between this rubric and those you likely see for state assessments. If we want our data to be "actionable," we won't focus on the composite score, the number you get when you add up the points from *all* categories. Instead, we'll recognize the importance of how students performed in individual areas: If Ella accurately answers the question, but has difficulty supporting her claim with evidence, you know your "action" should address strategies for choosing and using evidence.

CONSTRUCTED RESPONSE RUBRIC

Name _____ Task _____

	3 EXPERT	2 DEVELOPING	1 NOVICE	0 NO ATTEMPT OR INCORRECT	N/A
ANSWERS THE QUESTION (OFTEN AN INFERENCE)	Spot-on accuracy	Generally accurate	Close, approaching accuracy	Doesn't answer the question or answer is incorrect	
SUPPORTS THE ANSWER WITH TEXT EVIDENCE	Chooses the very best evidence and shows development	Evidence is relevant, but not the best; development may be unclear	Evidence is too general or a mix of relevant and irrelevant; no sense of development	Doesn't include evidence or evidence is irrelevant with no sense of development	
EXPLAINS THE EVIDENCE	Insightful and powerful explanation	Offers a reasonable, though limited explanation	Evidence mostly repeats the answer with no real extension	Does not include an explanation or explanation misses the point	
ORGANIZATION AND WRITTEN LANGUAGE	Logical organization with grade-appropriate writing	Mostly logical with writing that doesn't detract from content	Poorly organized with writing that makes it hard to understand content	Too short to evaluate writing or writing is unintelligible	
OTHER					
OTHER					

☐ Score for answering the question

☐ Score for selection and use of evidence

☐ Score for explanation of importance

☐ Score for organization and written language

Next steps for constructed response: _____

_____

Rubrics are great for teachers and can provide just what we need to move forward with instruction. They may be appropriate for older students to use, as well. But this type of measurement tool will probably be too complex for students in the lower intermediate grades, as there are just too many fine points to navigate. Instead, provide younger students with a checklist.

The checklist for constructed response is easy for students to use with only four criteria to evaluate. (Again, there's a place for an additional criterion if the teacher wishes to include one.) For students, it's a simple matter of deciding: *Does my answer have this thing or not?* Consider using this checklist for peer editing, too.

STUDENT CHECKLIST FOR CONSTRUCTED RESPONSE

Name _____ **Task** _____

☐ I answered the question and made a good inference if one was needed.

☐ I supported my answer with really good evidence, showing how the author *developed* the idea.

☐ I explained why this topic or evidence is important.

☐ My answer makes sense the way it is written. I was careful with spelling and punctuation.

Something else: _____

I think the best part of my answer is: _____
_____.

Something that was hard for me when I answered this question is: _____
_____

CHAPTER 3

GOOD QUESTIONS:

41 WAYS INTO A TEXT, INDEXED TO CONCEPTS AND TEACHING TOOLS

Truth: I love comprehension questions. I recognize this is excessively nerdy, and I do exercise some restraint in confessing it to my non-teacher friends. They all have hobbies like knitting, photography, and collecting unique fountain pens. I'm certain my fascination with questions we can ask kids about their reading would elicit looks of skepticism from these folks—or worse, pity. But as for me? I can't quell my enthusiasm for the many different lenses through which we can help students appreciate a text. That the Common Core brought to our classrooms an overabundance of new questions makes my heart sing.

I know that accessing a current list of key questions is not easy. We have anchor standards as well as grade-level benchmarks for each one, both of which should provide the guidance we need when crafting questions for our literacy curriculum. But when you look at the standard and then look at aligned assessment questions, you may be surprised by the way these new standards have been interpreted. After poring over countless questions on assessment websites, I think I've created a useful list of questions and offer it to you in a guide following this chapter: A Guide to the Questions, Concepts, and Teaching Tools In This Book.

Note that the coding system (1.1, 1.2, and so forth) is mine and is consistent with the way standards are labeled by the Common Core. For example, Standard 1 is about Evidence; Standard 2 relates to the Development of Ideas. The second number for each question refers to the number of the question under this standard. Some standards include more questions than others because these are areas where more focus is needed.

Refocusing Comprehension Questions

Teachers are good question-askers. In workshops, I'm often impressed with their creative thinking and the quality of their questions once we've talked about what's new in this regard, courtesy of the Common Core. What I also see, however, is their surprise that expectations for questions are different now. How can this be? New standards have been around for over a decade. We *start* with standards. We *end* with new assessments where students apply the standards. So, what happened to the thing in the *middle* that links standards to assessment—the *instruction*? That often appears to be business as usual for questioning strategies.

Despite updated literacy programs, close reading, and other practices that claim to be "cutting edge," lots of the questions I see and hear are the same ones that teachers have been asking forever. I encounter Depth of Knowledge 1 questions that check for basic understanding; Depth of Knowledge 2 questions where students apply rudimentary skills like sequencing events and summarizing; and a few Depth of Knowledge 3 questions that dig a little deeper into textual elements such as theme and character traits that call for inferences. In fact, these questions are good ones and teachers should continue to ask them. But there are more. So many more.

Could there be other questions beyond those I suggest? Of course—hundreds of them. But the list I offer is useful in two ways. First, these questions do appear with some regularity on high-stakes assessments. But even more importantly, these questions encourage kids to *think*. They're the kinds of questions you'll want to insert into your instruction not only for *writing* about reading, but for discussing beautiful literary works and important informational selections.

You'll find questions that are old favorites and others that are new and noteworthy. These are the same questions that are deconstructed with protocols for teaching students how to respond to them in Part II of this book. Take a few minutes to study the question list. What's familiar: questions you embed in your literacy instruction regularly? What's unfamiliar: questions with which your students have had minimal experience?

Seeing the Big Picture: What You Might Notice at First Glance

As you peruse these questions, also look for trends. What do you notice in both the content of the questions and the language used to ask them? What do they emphasize? Is there anything missing that you would expect to find here? To get this process started, I'll offer a few insights that you may recognize, too.

THERE ARE THREE STANDARDS BANDS

For clarification, we're talking about the College and Career Readiness Standards here, and the three "bands" under which the standards are categorized: *Key Ideas and Details; Craft and Structure;* and *Integration of Knowledge and Ideas.* These bands are important because they represent three very different lenses for analyzing a text: *What* the author is saying, *how* the author is saying it, and *why* the author is saying it. Dividing standards into these areas is our cue that we should be asking questions that fall within each of these bands.

How You Can Support Questions Across All Bands

Look closely at the questions you ask about any book you read with your students. Do they probe all three lenses for examining a text? They don't need to be the same questions as in our list, but they should address the *what, how,* and *why* of the author's words. You may notice that there's an imbalance in your questions, with more of them relating to *Key Ideas and Details* than to the other two areas. It does make sense that there will be lots of questions about *what* the author is saying. But there shouldn't be a huge imbalance. Next, look for opportunities to revise your questions to include all bands.

HEADINGS WITHIN EACH BAND ARE IDENTIFIED BY TEXT ELEMENT FIRST, NOT BY STANDARD

Yes, you teach *to* the standard, but you *teach* characterization, text features, word choice, and more. Standards are a means of organizing goals for students. But when we set our sights on Standard 2, or even more specifically, CCSS.ELA-LITERACY.RL.4.2, we get caught up in the rhetoric rather than in the rigor of learning what the standard represents. Know that when you focus your instruction on any of the headings under each band (Internal Text Organization, Author's Purpose, or any other question set), you *are* addressing an anchor standard. If you wish to sharpen your focus to the grade level application of that standard, search the Common Core English Language Arts Standards online.

How You Can Focus on Literacy Content and Standards

If you have a standards-based curriculum, then you will need to start with the standard. But within that standard, choose questions that are the best match for your text. One problem I see repeatedly is texts that don't work well with the questions teachers are asking. For example, for Standard 5, don't ask about the text structure of an informational source when the article contains several structures (like compare/contrast and main idea/details)—not a single overall structure.

What's NOT Here?

In addition to the features that distinguish these questions, there are some features you will notice are absent. And that's intentional.

THERE ARE NO "FLUFFY" QUESTIONS

By "fluffy" questions I mean those that are mostly subjective and therefore difficult to measure. Examples might be: *What is your favorite part of the story? Which character do you like best? What do you think about this problem?* It is true that these questions are text-based and that students would need to support their opinion with evidence. But they are not standards-based. With the limited time available for literacy instruction, we want to ask questions that require rigor from our students. "Fluffy" questions generally do not inspire rigor.

How You Can Minimize "Fluffy" Questions

These questions might be an adequate starting point for a discussion about a text, but don't warrant instruction in how to craft a written response. These aren't "bad" questions; we do care what students think about the books and other content they read. But if these are the only questions you're asking, they set the bar low for academic challenge.

THERE ARE NO QUESTIONS AIMED AT TEXT-TO-SELF CONNECTIONS OR OTHER METACOGNITIVE STRATEGIES

This was a surprising discovery upon the publication of the Common Core Standards given the over-the-top emphasis on personal connections and metacognitive strategies in general that dominated literacy instruction a decade ago. In the case of personal connections, we know where this led us—and it wasn't deeper into textual understanding. Personal connections often took students' thinking away from the text and down their own private Memory Lane: *One time I fell off my bike, too. I have a dog, but he's brown.*

Other metacognitive strategies such as visualizing and predicting are likewise absent from both the standards themselves and standards-based assessments. Here's why: Standards measure the *outcomes* of learning while strategies are the means by which students arrive at those outcomes. We don't measure process; we measure outcomes.

How You Can Honor Text-to-Self Connections and Other Metacognitive Strategies Without Overdoing It

It makes sense to model the use of comprehension strategies and to guide students to use these strategies themselves because we want students to be strategic readers. The difference between strategy instruction of the past and strategy instruction now is that instead of asking only "*What* did you picture in your mind?" We will follow that with "*How* did that picture in your mind help you to better understand the author's message?" In other words, strategies are a *means* to an end, not the end itself. Personal connections may be handled similarly, but there is an additional role for connections that will be explained later under *Explaining Importance*.

What We See When We Take a Deeper Look

Although we may find it hard to believe that comprehension questions could be very different from what we've been asking for decades, the reality is, they *are* different. Not all of them, of course, but enough to suggest important shifts in instruction and assessment. What kind of shifts? Recognizing the nuances in new questions will point us in the right direction.

WHEN SOMETHING OLD IS NEW AGAIN

Evidence and details are a good example of a surprising new spin on an area where we expected few surprises. In the past, *Key Ideas and Details* was familiar because we'd been asking basic comprehension questions since forever. Students *all* know the word "evidence" and "details." At least we could feel safe here. Then along came new questions that make even this comfort zone less comfortable—with queries like: *Which details are the most surprising?* Or, *What evidence best explains _____?* The difference here is that students are not just finding *relevant* evidence (a comparatively easy task). Now they need to choose evidence *selectively*, where the *quality* of the evidence is what matters. This becomes a *reasoning* question, not just a *retrieval* question, and requires deeper thinking.

How to Get Up-to-Speed with New Questions

The first order of business here is to read through the list of questions without assuming that you're up-to-speed on any of them. Look closely. Has anything changed? Next, incorporate the new questions into literacy discussions with your students. Part of the problem with students' written answers to comprehension questions is that questions they've never heard before are suddenly staring back at them on an important test. You can always *teach* the question later. But begin simply by asking it in a casual conversation.

SOME OF THIS STUFF REALLY IS NEW

One area where we'll want to be especially vigilant is *Craft and Structure*. You'll find questions that you've never seen before throughout all Standards bands. But you'll find them in the *Craft and Structure* band in unprecedented numbers. Even Vocabulary has undergone a transformation. No longer prioritizing unknown words, questions now focus a lot on word choice: how the author's precise choice of words conveys tone. There are also questions on the craft of writing, how an author includes devices like dialogue, gesture, and internal thoughts of a character to *show* rather than *tell*. How much do your students understand about the role of specific crafts? Most troublesome might be questions connected to the internal organization of a text—for example, how paragraphs or stanzas are connected to each other. Can we honestly say we've addressed questions like these with our students?

As we acknowledge uncharted territory, we should also cue the third Standards band, *Integration of Knowledge and Ideas*. First, there are the challenges of Standard 8: focused on the validity of reasoning and the sufficiency and relevance of evidence. What? Have you ever asked this at your grade level? You may have asked questions related to integrating texts, though a few of these would be hard to anticipate—for instance, *Which source does a better job of explaining _____?*

What to Keep in Mind When You're Introducing New Questions

In many cases, it's not just the *question* that is new, but the *concept* upon which the question is based. This will be true for questions related to things like internal structure, author's craft, and critical thinking. It will be useless to ask these until students understand the concept. The scaffolds for specific questions in Part II of this book will give you a place to begin.

BEWARE THE LANGUAGE OF SOME QUESTIONS

Sometimes it's not the question that is difficult, it's the way the question is stated that makes it hard for students to understand. You'll notice this confusion in the question *What is the central idea of _____?* When I share this question with students (as I did in the model lesson), students tell me they've never heard the term "central idea." We take time to discuss it, and I point out that other labels could have been used instead: theme, main idea, lesson, moral, and more. Academic language can get in the way of students' constructed responses as much as lack of comprehension. Recognize this and teach accordingly.

How to Help Students Interpret the Language of Questions

Read questions before you introduce them to students and be proactive about addressing words that could potentially cause confusion. Teach students to read questions and do the same. Post anchor charts with academic language, both synonyms and definitions.

"THE AUTHOR" SHOWS UP IN A LOT OF QUESTIONS

Where is the flashback in the story and what is the most likely reason the author included it? What is the author's point of view about _____? Why do you think the author wrote this as a poem _____? Suddenly, the author is *everywhere* in standards-based questions. Why is that? This is another way to up the ante for inferential and critical thinking. We are not simply asking *Where is the flashback?* (a straightforward matter of identifying a literary device). We're not even just requiring students to explain the information in the flashback (still a basic comprehension task). Rather, we want students to consider the purpose for including it. This is an excellent question as readers must now consider the flashback (or whatever) in the context of the full text. In the case of the source written as a *poem*, students need to access their knowledge of genres to respond critically. For the question about determining the author's point of view in a text (that's not written in the first person), what tone words lead you to your answer?

How to Help Students Get Inside the Author's Head

The key to helping students respond well to author's intent is to make sure they're approaching their reading with the right mindset. Meaning begins with the words the author has placed on the page. While readers bring their own thinking to a text as they interpret it (and they should!), it's the *author's* thinking that must be the starting point. You can't interpret what you don't understand. And understanding comes not only from *what* an author says, but *why* they are saying it. A serious consequence of all that emphasis we once placed on personal connections is that students put too much value on their own thoughts without first recognizing what the author valued. We need to build a better understanding of why the author's intent is so critical if we want to educate critical thinkers.

What other patterns or points did you notice as you perused the list of questions? The more nuances you recognize and the more you contemplate ways to address them, the more your students will be prepared to produce quality constructed responses. But we can still do more. We can provide hands-on scaffolds that will streamline teaching and optimize learning. What kinds of scaffolds? Find out in the next chapter.

A GUIDE TO THE QUESTIONS, CONCEPTS, AND TEACHING TOOLS IN THIS BOOK

For each standards-based comprehension concept you wish to teach, note the aligned question and the anchor charts or checklists you can use to build students' understanding through modeling and practicing.

KEY IDEAS AND DETAILS

STANDARD AND CONCEPT	QUESTION	TOOLS FOR ANALYTICAL READING
Standard 1: Evidence **Concept:** Finding Surprising Details	1.1: Which details are the most surprising?	• Anchor Chart 1: Finding Surprising or Helpful Details in a Story or Poem • Anchor Chart 2: Finding Surprising or Helpful Details in an Informational Text
Standard 1: Evidence **Concept:** Finding Helpful Details	1.2: Which details were the most helpful in figuring out _____?	• Anchor Chart 1: Finding Surprising or Helpful Details in a Story or Poem • Anchor Chart 2: Finding Surprising or Helpful Details in an Informational Text
Standard 1: Evidence **Concept:** Explaining Importance	1.3: Why is the evidence important?	• Anchor Chart 3: Explaining Importance in Fiction and Nonfiction* *There is a minilesson and an anchor chart for this question because it is a key component of many responses. Because it is never a standalone question, there is no cue card, answer frame, or sample response.
Standard 2: Developing Ideas **Concept:** Paraphrasing	2.1: Paraphrase this [paragraph] to show its meaning in your own words.	• Checklist 1: Paraphrasing
Standard 2: Developing Ideas **Concept:** Proving a Stated Central Idea	2.2: How does the author develop the idea of _____?	• Anchor Chart 1: Finding Surprising or Helpful Details in a Story or Poem • Anchor Chart 2: Finding Surprising or Helpful Details in an Informational Text • Anchor Chart 3: Explaining Importance in Fiction and Nonfiction

STANDARD AND CONCEPT	QUESTION	TOOLS FOR ANALYTICAL READING
Standard 2: Developing Ideas **Concept:** Inferring a Central Idea	2.3: What is the central idea/theme of _____ and how does the author develop it?	• Anchor Chart 4: Topics and Central Ideas for Narrative Fiction and Nonfiction • Anchor Chart 1: Finding Surprising or Helpful Details in a Story or Poem • Anchor Chart 2: Finding Surprising or Helpful Details in an Informational Text • Anchor Chart 3: Explaining Importance in Fiction and Nonfiction
Standard 2: Developing Ideas **Concept:** Identifying a Main Idea in an Informational Text	2.4: What is the main idea of this [paragraph] and how does the author develop it?	• Anchor Chart 2: Finding Surprising or Helpful Details in an Informational Text • Anchor Chart 3: Explaining Importance in Fiction and Nonfiction
Standard 2: Developing Ideas **Concept:** Summarizing a Story with Story Parts	2.5: Briefly summarize this story including only the key points.	• Anchor Chart 17: Analyzing Story Parts • Anchor Chart 4: Topics and Central Ideas for Narrative Fiction and Nonfiction • Anchor Chart 3: Explaining Importance in Fiction and Nonfiction
Standard 2: Developing Ideas **Concept:** Drawing a Conclusion	2.6: What conclusion can you draw about [character, problem, etc.]?	• Anchor Chart 1: Finding Surprising or Helpful Details in a Story or Poem • Anchor Chart 2: Finding Surprising or Helpful Details in an Informational Text • Anchor Chart 3: Explaining Importance in Fiction and Nonfiction
Standard 3: Characters and Other Text Elements **Concept:** Character Traits and Feelings	3.1: What character trait (or feeling) does [character] mainly show in this story?	• Anchor Chart 5: Positive Character Traits and Shades of Meaning • Anchor Chart 6: Negative Character Traits and Shades of Meaning • Anchor Chart 7: Positive Character Feelings and Shades of Meaning • Anchor Chart 8: Negative Character Feelings and Shades of Meaning • Anchor Chart 3: Explaining Importance in Fiction and Nonfiction

STANDARD AND CONCEPT	QUESTION	TOOLS FOR ANALYTICAL READING
Standard 3: Characters and Other Text Elements **Concept:** Character Attitudes and Author's Tone	3.2: What is the character's attitude, and how does it make a difference?	• Anchor Chart 9: Positive Character Attitudes and Author's Tone • Anchor Chart 10: Negative Character Attitudes and Author's Tone
Standard 3: Characters and Other Text Elements **Concept:** Character Motivation	3.3: What motivated [character] to _____?	• Anchor Chart 11: Analyzing Character Motivations • Anchor Chart 3: Explaining Importance in Fiction and Nonfiction
Standard 3: Characters and Other Text Elements **Concept:** Character Relationships	3.4: What is the relationship between [Character A] and [Character B]?	• Anchor Chart 12: Analyzing Character Relationships • Anchor Chart 3: Explaining Importance in Fiction and Nonfiction
Standard 3: Characters and Other Text Elements **Concept:** Character's or Author's Point of View	3.5: What is [Character's / Author's] point of view about _____? How does the character (or author) show this?	• Anchor Chart 13: Reasons for a Character's Behavior • Anchor Chart 3: Explaining Importance in Fiction and Nonfiction
Standard 3: Characters and Other Text Elements **Concept:** Character Differences	3.6: What are the most important differences between [Character A] and [Character B]?	• Anchor Chart 13: Reasons for a Character's Behavior • Anchor Chart 14: Comparing Characters
Standard 3: Characters and Other Text Elements **Concept:** Relationship Between Text Elements	3.7: What is the relationship between [the setting] and [the problem] in _____?	• Anchor Chart 15: How Setting Matters in a Story or Real-Life Event • Anchor Chart: 16: Analyzing the Problem • Anchor Chart 3: Explaining Importance in Fiction and Nonfiction

CRAFT AND STRUCTURE

STANDARD AND CONCEPT	QUESTION	TOOLS FOR ANALYTICAL READING
Standard 4: Author's Craft **Concept:** Determining Word Meaning	4.1: What does [word] mean and what clue in the text helped you to understand it?	• No anchor charts are needed for this question
Standard 4: Author's Craft **Concept:** Choosing Precise Words	4.2: What word might the author use to make the meaning in this [sentence] clearer?	• No anchor charts are needed for this question
Standard 4: Author's Craft **Concept:** Author's Tone	4.3: What words create the tone in this [paragraph]? What is the tone?	• Anchor Chart 9: Positive Character Attitudes and Author's Tone • Anchor Chart 10: Negative Character Attitudes and Author's Tone
Standard 4: Author's Craft **Concept:** Literary Techniques	4.4: What author's craft (like description, dialogue, internal dialogue, and gesture) does the author use in this [part of the story] and why do you think the author included it?	• Anchor Chart 18: Analyzing Author's Craft in Narrative Text
Standard 4: Author's Craft **Concept:** Figurative Language	4.5: What figurative language (like simile, metaphor, personification, idiom, or hyperbole) does the author use in this [paragraph] and why do you think the author chose it?	• Anchor Chart 19: Analyzing Figurative Language
Standard 4: Author's Craft **Concept:** Genre Elements: Fable	4.6: What elements of a [fable] did you find in this text? Find at least two elements and explain how the author uses them.	• Anchor Chart 20: Analyzing a Fable
Standard 4: Author's Craft **Concept:** Genre Elements: Poem	4.7: Why do you think the author wrote this as a [poem]?	• Anchor Chart 21: Analyzing a Poem

STANDARD AND CONCEPT	QUESTION	TOOLS FOR ANALYTICAL READING
Standard 5: Text Structure **Concept:** Text Features	5.1: What is this text feature and what is the most likely reason the author included it?	• Anchor Chart 22: Analyzing Informational Text Features
Standard 5: Text Structure **Concept:** Text Structures	5.2: What text structure did the author choose for writing [about this topic] and what is the most likely reason the author chose it?	• Anchor Chart 23: Analyzing Informational Text Structures
Standard 5: Text Structure **Concept:** Kind of Information in a Passage	5.3: What kind of information does the author provide in [paragraph A] and why does the author include it?	• Anchor Chart 24: Analyzing the Kind of Information an Author Includes in a [Paragraph]
Standard 5: Text Structure **Concept:** Connection Between [Paragraphs]	5.4: How does [paragraph A] connect to [paragraph B]?	• Anchor Chart 25: Analyzing How Parts of a Text Fit Together
Standard 5: Text Structure **Concept:** Beginning and Ending of a Story	5.5: Why did the author choose to begin/end the story with this [paragraph]?	• Anchor Chart 26: Analyzing How an Author Begins a Story • Anchor Chart 27: Analyzing How an Author Ends a Story
Standard 5: Text Structure **Concept:** Flashback that Provides Background	5.6: Where is the flashback in the story and why did the author most likely include it?	• Anchor Chart 28: Analyzing a Flashback • Anchor Chart 3: Explaining Importance in Fiction and Nonfiction
Standard 5: Text Structure **Concept 5:** Backstory that Provides Context	5.7: What is the backstory for this [story], and why did the author most likely include it?	• Anchor Chart 29: Analyzing a Backstory • Anchor Chart 3: Explaining Importance in Fiction and Nonfiction

STANDARD AND CONCEPT	QUESTION	TOOLS FOR ANALYTICAL READING
Standard 5: Text Structure **Concept:** Quote that Begins a [Chapter]	5.8: Why do you think the author included this quote from another author at the beginning of this [chapter]?	• Anchor Chart 30: Analyzing a Quote from Another Author at the Beginning of a Book or Chapter • Anchor Chart 3: Explaining Importance in Fiction and Nonfiction
Standard 6: Purpose and point of View **Concept:** Different Point of View	6.1: How would this story change if it were told from [new narrator's] point of view?	• Anchor Chart 7: Positive Character Feelings and Shades of Meaning • Anchor Chart 8: Negative Character Feelings and Shades of Meaning • Anchor Chart 9: Positive Character Attitudes and Author's Tone • Anchor Chart 10: Negative Character Attitudes and Author's Tone • Anchor Chart 11: Analyzing Character Motivations
Standard 6: Purpose and Point of View **Concept:** Reader's Point of View	6.2: What is your point of view about _____, and how is it the same or different from the point of view of the author?	• Checklist 2: Defending a Point of View • Anchor Chart 2: Finding Surprising or Helpful Details in an Informational Text • Anchor Chart 3: Explaining Importance in Fiction and Nonfiction
Standard 6: Purpose and Point of View **Concept:** Author's Purpose for Including Particular Information	6.3: What was the author's purpose for including this [paragraph/sentence]?	• Anchor Chart 31: Analyzing an Author's Purpose for Including a Particular Paragraph or Sentence • Anchor Chart 3: Explaining Importance in Fiction and Nonfiction

STANDARD AND CONCEPT	QUESTION	TOOLS FOR ANALYTICAL READING
Standard 7: Nonprint Texts **Concept:** Analyzing a Video	7.1: How did this video add to your understanding of _____?	• Anchor Chart 32: Analyzing a Video
Standard 7: Nonprint Texts **Concept:** Analyzing an Illustration or Photograph	7.2: Why do you think the author included this illustration (or photograph)?	• Anchor Chart 33: Analyzing a Photograph or Illustration
Standard 8: Relevance and Sufficiency of Evidence **Concept:** Finding Relevant Details	8.1: Which details from [the text] are relevant to the argument that _____?	• Anchor Chart 2: Finding Surprising or Helpful Details in an Informational Text • Anchor Chart 3: Explaining Importance in Fiction and Nonfiction
Standard 8: Relevance and Eufficiency of Evidence **Concept:** Adding Relevant Details	8.2: What additional evidence for _____ could the author have included to make the argument more convincing?	• Checklist 3: Critiquing an Explanation • Anchor Chart 3: Explaining Importance in Fiction and Nonfiction
Standard 9: Connections Between Texts **Concept:** Critiquing Sources	9.1: Which source does a better job of explaining _____? Cite specific evidence to support your answer.	• Checklist 3: Critiquing an Explanation • Anchor Chart 3: Explaining Importance in Fiction and Nonfiction
Standard 9: Connections Between Texts **Concept:** Integrating Multiple Sources	9.2: Explain how each of the selections you read about [topic] could be useful to someone writing about this topic.	• Anchor Chart 34: Integrating Information from Multiple Sources • Anchor Chart 3: Explaining Importance in Fiction and Nonfiction

STANDARD AND CONCEPT	QUESTION	TOOLS FOR ANALYTICAL READING
Standard 9: Connections Between Texts **Concept:** Writing Fiction from Nonfiction Sources	9.3: Use the information from these [two] sources to write a diary entry from your point of view, imagining that you are personally experiencing the situation identified in these sources. Be sure to include details from the informational sources you read.	• Checklist 4: Writing a Diary Entry
Standard 9: Connections Between Texts **Concept:** Comparing Texts Based on Central Idea or Other Text Element	9.4: Identify the central idea in Source #1 and Source #2. Then compare and contrast the way the author develops the central idea in each of the sources.	• Anchor Chart 4: Topics and Central Ideas for Narrative Fiction and Nonfiction • Anchor Chart 35: Comparing Similarities and Differences Between Literary Texts • Anchor Chart 36: Comparing Similarities and Differences Between Informational Texts • Anchor Chart 3: Explaining Importance in Fiction and Nonfiction

...her hair. "Just like you did with the mirror you looked at

...ing right?" she asked back. I was laughing really hard because that

...son. The good thing is that no harsh feelings get caught in the action.

...the best for me; they want me to go to school and graduate with a

...perfect studying. A regular basis please they repeat to me is

...the monetary problems to us" something I can never consider.

...hair stylist 6 days a week. She studied that on one of the best

...the Dominican Republic at the time which was around 20 years

...r's a good thing. My dad is a sales man for a new company

...focus on high-quality windows that are tough enough to

...on the ocean areas which are the most touristic-based

I want, what I dream of, and no matter how big or

...o them and to never let go because dreams are

...t our dreams can become true makes us

...hange, our dreams change too. My dad and I

...grew up. I was 14 at the time. He simply

...He looked at me and said "Fidel, I know,

...him the you-think-I'm-stupid look

..."I said. He took a deep breath and

...o Domingo, the capital

...r her and my dad said in Spanish "careful

...to achieve

...r well on tests

...all. I applaud him

...ports, and a social life. He

...at he had gotten accepted to almost

...our class with a 4.2 GPA! On the night

...students received scholarships for the

...ip he got was for $500. The night

...ip he wasn't going to get any more

...Then, the final name was c

...figures. I

PART II

Hands-on Support
for **Reading** and **Understanding**

CHAPTER 4

MINILESSONS FOR ANALYTICAL READING

Developing analytical readers is hard. We recognize the importance of analyzing text, but the perception much of the time is that it's not teachable. Students either have the intellectual capacity to reason analytically—or they don't. We believe that there's not much we can do except point out that certain textual elements need analysis: things like character traits, cause and effect, theme, and more. The author provides clues to meaning but doesn't state the trait or theme directly. Hence, the need for analysis.

In the virtual lesson described in Chapter 1, I supported analytical reading through the anchor chart *during* my lesson because I didn't have another way of handling it. (I wasn't coming back the next day.) But if you're teaching your own class where you meet with groups regularly (in person, or online at a distance), you could be more planful about how you get started with analysis. Teach the concept itself as a minilesson *before* students need to apply it to answer a question. This could be a whole class or small group lesson, depending on your students' needs, and may take 20–30 minutes.

A good analytical reading lesson should include: An explanation of the comprehension concept, a text to model the concept, and tools for students to practice applying the concept. Here's how these features will apply to lessons in this book. (You'll get to the actual question soon enough. But right now, focus on the comprehension *concept*.)

Explain the Concept

While your eventual goal is for students to be able to answer a specified comprehension question, you will achieve that goal by helping them understand the related comprehension concept (or concepts). So, that is the aim of your lesson: teaching the concept.

Good lessons begin with a good explanation, and a good explanation includes not only *what* students are expected to do, but *how* they will do it successfully.

All explanations in this book are written in conversational language that will make sense to students in the intermediate grades. You can read the explanations aloud or students can read them with you. Each explanation contains some standard guidelines, but also a few less obvious tips that I've recognized over the years. Sometimes it's these small points that make the biggest difference to students' comfort level with a new concept. Feel free to add your own hints that lead you to success with a concept, too. Regardless of how you present your explanation, build in plenty of time to discuss it.

Choose Texts Matched to the Concept

When students apply a concept, you'll want to use authentic short texts for modeling and practicing, sources such as articles, short stories, poems, picture books, or excerpts from longer pieces. Short texts are best for explicit lessons because all textual components are present in a few paragraphs or a couple of pages. This way, students don't get bogged down by the quantity of material they are expected to read.

Different concepts (and questions) are aligned to different kinds of texts. Each minilesson identifies criteria you'll want to consider for the concept central to the question your students will answer. Try to provide students with a balanced diet of many types of reading content: fiction, nonfiction, poetry (both classic and modern), and even nonprint texts like video clips, photographs, or illustrations.

Provide Practice with Tools

Students need hands-on tools to practice new learning—in this case, comprehension concepts—and in this book these tools take the form of anchor charts and checklists, all of which are interactive. The actual charts and checklists are provided in Chapter 5: Tools for Analytical Reading. But these tools are identified as part of each minilesson so you will know exactly what chart or checklist to access in Chapter 5.

Which details are most surprising?

The kind of details you find in a story or poem are different from the details you find in an informational source. This means that the texts you choose and the way you explain concept will be different, as well as the tools for modeling and practicing.

EXPLAIN THE CONCEPT:
FINDING SURPRISING DETAILS IN A STORY OR POEM

To recognize *surprising* details, you first need to understand where to look for evidence. Then you can decide if the detail surprises you—and why. The kinds of evidence you'll find in a story or poem are different from the evidence in an informational text. In a story you typically meet characters facing a problem and attempting to solve it. You build expectations for their behavior and the way the situation may play out based on four kinds of evidence:

- Description of the character, problem, or setting
- A character's inside thoughts
- A character's words
- A character's small actions or gestures

Sometimes the story moves along exactly as we expect, with characters saying and doing things that are predictable. But other times, characters behave in ways we don't anticipate. Or problems take a surprising turn. For example, the narrator of a story might have behaved boldly in the past. He announces to his friends that he's not at all worried about today's math test. But his "inside thought" is: *Oh, no, I forgot to study! I'm doomed!* You are surprised because you didn't expect this character to feel insecure.

EXPLAIN THE CONCEPT:
FINDING SURPRISING DETAILS IN AN INFORMATIONAL SOURCE

Finding surprising evidence in an informational text is a different matter entirely. You won't have characters and a problem to follow, but you'll have plenty of other kinds of details like dates, facts, quotes from experts, and more. One important thing to keep in mind about evidence in informational sources is that it must be *reliable*. That means you need to be able to trust it to be true. If you read a "fact" that you can find in several sources, you can probably trust it. If someone is sharing their personal experience, that *might* be trustworthy. But remember that this is only *one* person's experience. When you read about an informational topic, *do* look for details that are surprising, but always ask yourself: Can I trust this surprising detail to be true? Why or why not?

CHOOSE TEXTS

Choose literary texts for this question that don't always follow the "rules." For example, maybe the fairy-tale princess will decide in the end not marry the prince. Maybe the character who looked like the "good guy" for several chapters is actually the one who committed the crime. Maybe the last line of a poem delivers a zinger that you weren't expecting. The poet Jack Prelutsky is famous for surprise endings that the reader didn't see coming—and leave readers chuckling.

Surprising details in an informational text are facts or claims you didn't know before. This may present a problem if you choose an article where students have lots of background knowledge. "Nothing surprised me here," a third grader announced one afternoon when I was doing a lesson in his class on the platypus. "I've read every book in the library with information about platypuses." Perhaps we should rephrase the question: *What information in this text did the author think would surprise us?*

The following tools provide practice with concepts important for answering Question 1.1.

PROVIDE PRACTICE USING TOOLS IN CHAPTER 5

- Anchor Chart 1: Finding Surprising or Helpful Details in a Story or Poem
- Anchor Chart 2: Finding Surprising or Helpful Details in an Informational Text

Which details were the most helpful in figuring out _____?

EXPLAIN THE CONCEPT: FINDING HELPFUL DETAILS

This is a question you'll often want to consider when you're trying to figure something out—like solving a mystery or answering a riddle: Who committed the crime? What animal is the author describing with a series of clues? How will this story probably end? You will need good detective skills to succeed in these situations because the author provides lots of details, some of which are more helpful than others. Good readers examine all possible clues carefully, noticing even small bits of information that might seem unimportant at first glance. What could this detail mean? How do all the details add up? At some point, a lightbulb in your brain flashes: "Aha, I've got it!" you exclaim. What was that detail that completed the puzzle for you? Why was it so helpful? Good reading detectives recognize why a particular detail mattered to them. That's what we want to consider as we respond to this question.

CHOOSE TEXTS

When you want students to truly value evidence, provide them with a mystery to read. Solving a mystery hinges on finding evidence and putting the pieces together. My favorite author for kid-size mysteries is Chris Van Allsburg, because his mysteries are written as picture books with wonderful illustrations that provide additional clues. I especially like *The Stranger, The Wretched Stone,* and *The Mysteries of Harris Burdick.* These stories are as intriguing as they are clever. But almost any read-aloud story can be made mysterious. Stop a couple of pages from the end and ask, "What happens? How do you think the story ends?" If students have paid close attention to the clues, they'll be able to come pretty close to the author's ending.

The following tools provide practice with concepts important for answering Question 1.2.

PROVIDE PRACTICE USING TOOLS IN CHAPTER 5

- Anchor Chart 1: Finding Surprising or Helpful Details in a Story or Poem
- Anchor Chart 2: Finding Surprising or Helpful Details in an Informational Text

Why is the evidence important?

EXPLAIN THE CONCEPT: EXPLAINING IMPORTANCE

Explaining the importance of evidence will apply to *many* questions, not just one. The tricky thing is that constructed response questions don't usually ask you to explain why the evidence you've chosen is important, but you'll get a better score if you remember to include it. Explaining importance makes sense because you should have a good reason for selecting your details. Often, this explanation will go at the end of your response, although you could explain why each detail is important as you write it.

Explaining importance does not mean restating your claim. You need to connect your final thought to the text, but you also need to go beyond the story or the information itself to explain why what you've read matters. To do this, you could consider insights related to personal connections, why the message is important to other people as well as to you, how other people might react to the message, or the more general life lesson. You don't need to write a lot to explain importance. A couple of sentences should get the job done.

CHOOSE TEXTS

There are no texts specific to this question because explaining importance is a component of answering any question.

The following tool provides practice with the concept of explaining importance: very important for answering many questions.

PROVIDE PRACTICE USING TOOLS IN CHAPTER 5

- Anchor Chart 3: Explaining Importance in Fiction and Nonfiction

Paraphrase this [paragraph] to show its meaning in your own words.

EXPLAIN THE CONCEPT: PARAPHRASING

When you paraphrase, you put something in your own words, showing that you understood the meaning of what you read. You might paraphrase a sentence or a paragraph, or perhaps a stanza of a poem. Readers are seldom asked to paraphrase a full text like a story or news article. When you paraphrase, use as few words as possible from the original text, but be sure not to change the meaning. Some words, like names, will stay the same. You want your paraphrased version to be accurate, but to sound more like *you* and less like the author who wrote it originally. It will be about the same length as the original, as you are not writing a summary. When a question asks you to paraphrase, you do not need to explain the importance as you do with most other constructed response questions.

CHOOSE TEXTS

This is an excellent question to monitor basic comprehension and works well with short portions of any genre of text. Choose a passage with sufficient complexity for the students in your group, or there won't be any reason for them to paraphrase it. Consider using a poem from authors such as Robert Frost, Emily Dickinson, or Robert Louis Stevenson, as students need more exposure to the language demands in these classic works. Specify a page, paragraph, stanza, or even a single sentence and ask students to say it in their own words. Unlike a summary, the goal for paraphrasing is not brevity but clarity and accuracy.

The following tool provides practice with the concept of paraphrasing, important for answering Question 2.1.

PROVIDE PRACTICE USING TOOLS IN CHAPTER 5

- Checklist 1: Paraphrasing

How does the author develop the idea of

_____?

EXPLAIN THE CONCEPT: PROVING A STATED CENTRAL IDEA

This is an easy question because it gives you the inference, the answer itself. All you need to do is find the evidence to prove it, and then (as usual) explain the importance of your evidence. The key to a good response for this question will be the quality of the evidence you choose. You need the most useful evidence. It must prove what you say it's proving, and there must be *enough* evidence. For informational text, the evidence must also be *reliable*, from a source you trust.

CHOOSE TEXTS

This is an easy question for students because the central idea (or other text component such as character trait) is given to them in the question. Their job is simply to defend the claim with supporting evidence. For this reason, this is an excellent question for less mature readers, which may also mean choosing less complex sources, either literary or informational.

The following tools provide practice with concepts important for answering Question 2.2.

PROVIDE PRACTICE USING TOOLS IN CHAPTER 5

- Anchor Chart 1: Finding Surprising or Helpful Details in a Story or Poem
- Anchor Chart 2: Finding Surprising or Helpful Details in an Informational Text
- Anchor Chart 3: Explaining Importance in Fiction and Nonfiction

What is the central idea/theme of _____ and how does the author develop it?

EXPLAIN THE CONCEPT: INFERRING A CENTRAL IDEA

Your answer to this question will be the same as your answer to the question where the central idea is provided—except that for this question, you'll need to figure out the central idea yourself. It will be important to think hard about the central idea and identify it correctly, or it will be impossible to write a good response. Start looking for the central idea right from the beginning of the text. Sometimes readers wait until they have finished a story or article to think about its message. That's too late! Look for clues as early as the first paragraph. Make a prediction about the central idea and tweak it as you continue reading. By the time you reach the last paragraph, you should have a clear idea of both the central idea and the evidence to support it.

Keep in mind too the difference between a *topic* and a *central idea*. The *topic* an author writes about can usually be stated in a single word (like family, kindness, or friendship), but the *central idea* is a statement or opinion *about* the topic, expressed in a sentence or phrase. It is the message the author is trying to send readers and may answer the question, "What lesson does the main character learn in the story?" It could be something like: Family members support each other. Or: It's important to show kindness toward animals.

Remember that other words might be used instead of central idea for this question: theme, lesson, moral, message, and others. Regardless of the term, your answer will be the same. To show its development, you need details from the beginning, middle, and end of the text—kind of like a short summary.

Also note that topics and central ideas related to expository nonfiction are more specific to individual sources and less easily generalized. There are *thousands* of possible topics and central ideas—way too many to try to list on an Anchor Chart. If the source is expository, look at the title, headings, and subheadings to help you figure out the topic and central ideas. The first and last paragraphs may help you, too. There may be several central (main) ideas within a topic.

CHOOSE TEXTS

This question is useful for both fiction and nonfiction, although it is asked more frequently for literary text, including poetry. Most complex literary texts do not state the central idea, calling for an inference. Informational sources often have several central ideas, sometimes identified through their headings and subheadings. The best sources when asking this question will have lots of details so students can easily show the *development* of ideas. Selecting texts with themes students have experienced will lead to greater success. For example, picking a poem about the perils of bullying will resonate more with third graders than a passage about the perils of falling in love.

The following tools provide practice with concepts important for answering Question 2.3.

PROVIDE PRACTICE USING TOOLS IN CHAPTER 5

- Anchor Chart 4: Topics and Central Ideas for Narrative Fiction and Nonfiction
- Anchor Chart 1: Finding Surprising or Helpful Details in a Story or Poem
- Anchor Chart 2: Finding Surprising or Helpful Details in an Informational Text
- Anchor Chart 3: Explaining Importance in Fiction and Nonfiction

What is the main idea of this [paragraph] and how does the author develop it?

EXPLAIN THE CONCEPT:
IDENTIFYING A MAIN IDEA IN AN INFORMATIONAL TEXT

Sometimes questions about main idea in an informational source will focus on the whole selection, especially if it's a short one like an article. But more often, you will be asked to identify the main idea in a part of a text, perhaps a specific paragraph or the information under one heading or subheading.

Always look first to see if the main idea is stated. The most likely places to find a stated main idea will be the first or last sentence in a paragraph or short passage. In a full text, you might find a main idea statement in the introductory paragraph or in the conclusion. Be sure to pick the sentence that fits best with *all* the details in the passage or selection.

If the main idea is not stated, you will need to figure it out, and unfortunately there isn't a chart to help you. In stories, some themes are common, and they repeat over and over. But in informational texts, the main idea in every paragraph may be different. Even if the main idea is not stated, there will be clues. Does the passage begin with a question? If so, the answer to that question will probably be the main idea. What does the author spend the most time explaining? If it takes up the most space, it must be an important idea. Are there key words in the title or heading? Are there bolded words? These can lead you to a main idea, too.

Once you've found or inferred your main idea, there's still work ahead. What evidence can you find that supports the main idea? With informational text, *developing* an idea is not usually a sequence of events. However, you should be able to locate more than one detail that proves your point. You should also conclude your response by explaining why people should care about this topic.

CHOOSE TEXTS

This question is typically asked about informational text, although it could also apply to passages within a literary selection: What is the main idea in this paragraph (or under this heading)? Avoid asking for a single main idea about a lengthy informational source. There are usually many big ideas included in a full informational text, and a main idea statement that covers all of it may be too broad to be meaningful, more of a topic than a main idea. For example, "too broad" statements might include: *This article is about sharks.* Or, *This chapter is about the Battle of Trenton during the American Revolution.* The best sources when asking this question will have an expository format with bolded headings and paragraphs that are well constructed with topic sentences and supporting details.

The following tools provide practice with concepts important for answering Question 2.4.

PROVIDE PRACTICE USING TOOLS IN CHAPTER 5

- Anchor Chart 2: Finding Surprising or Helpful Details in an Informational Text
- Anchor Chart 3: Explaining Importance in Fiction and Nonfiction

Briefly summarize this story including only the key points.

EXPLAIN THE CONCEPT:
SUMMARIZING A STORY WITH STORY PARTS

A summary is a brief account of something with only the key points included. Although you could be asked to summarize any kind of text, this is often a task related to a story: *Summarize the fable "The Tortoise and the Hare."* Write a brief summary of Chapter Three in *Because of Winn-Dixie*. A summary should be *brief* compared to the full text, and it should include just the most important points, not the less significant details. Sometimes it's hard to decide what is important and what is not. One hint to keep in mind is that the important points are usually *actions* while the less important ones are *descriptions*. For instance, you would probably include *Cinderella lost her slipper on the way home from the ball*. You would omit *Cinderella's slipper was made of glass*.

There are many ways to summarize, although the question will not always include the word *summarize*. Instead it might say, "Show the *development* of the central idea (or something else) in the story." Watch for the word *develop* or *development* because it is really asking you to summarize.

Summarizing with story parts is a good strategy for fairy tales, picture books, or other narrative selections where you are reading the whole story. For this format, you'll need to think about what happens at the beginning, middle, and end of the story and how all the story parts work together: characters, setting, problem, actions, outcome, ending.

Follow these steps for summarizing a story with this format:
- Tell what happens at the <u>beginning</u> of the story. This should include the characters, the setting, and the problem.
- Tell what happens in the <u>middle</u> of the story. This should include actions including roadblocks to solving the problem, or steps to finding a solution.
- Tell what happens at the <u>end</u> of the story. This should include the way the problem is solved (or the outcome) and the ending.

This is not the only summary format, however. Three other summary strategies you might want to consider are:

- **[Somebody] wanted** _____**, but** _____**, so** _____**.**
  Use this strategy for very short stories (such as fables) that have a problem and a solution, and not many details in between.

- **Sequential Summary: First, next, then, after that, finally**
  Use this strategy if there is a logical progression of actions or steps within the text, but not a problem and a solution. This might include biographies, personal narratives, and memoirs. Or it could work for informational sources that explain issues with causes and effects. It could even apply to a single chapter or portion of a text (usually a story).

- **Main ideas and details**
  Use this strategy for short informational pieces like articles or essays that are set up as a series of paragraphs.

CHOOSE TEXTS

We can make summarizing a story more manageable by teaching with short texts. Traditional literature such as fairy tales, myths, and legends work well because they all have a problem–solution format with a sequential storyline. Although there are many summarizing strategies, it is the format for summarizing with story parts that is explained here. This means you will need to choose a full text where all story parts are included. An excerpt from a longer story won't work because it may not include the solution to the problem or other key story elements—which would make it impossible for students to use this format.

The following tools provide practice with concepts important for answering Question 2.5.

PROVIDE PRACTICE USING TOOLS IN CHAPTER 5

- Anchor Chart 17: Analyzing Story Parts
- Anchor Chart 4: Topics and Central Ideas for Narrative Fiction and Nonfiction
- Anchor Chart 3: Explaining Importance in Fiction and Nonfiction

What conclusion can you draw about [character, problem, etc.]?

EXPLAIN THE CONCEPT: DRAWING A CONCLUSION:

"Drawing conclusions" is an odd term because it doesn't mean what you may think it means at first glance. You are not *drawing* anything, no markers or crayons required. It also has a slightly different meaning from writing the "conclusion" to an essay or other piece of writing—which is typically the final paragraph or last few sentences that tie the piece together. Rather, when you "draw a conclusion," you make an inference based on all the available evidence. You look at the clues and figure something out that the author has *shown* you but doesn't tell you directly. A good conclusion does more than describe an event. It explains the meaning of the event, or something else in a text. It might answer the question *Why* did something happen—like *why* did a character behave in a certain way? It could answer other questions, too.

When you see this question, it doesn't always lead you to the *central* idea. But it should lead you to an *important* idea, or it wouldn't make sense to ask the question at all. For this response, you'll want your answer to include as much evidence as possible in order to convince readers of your conclusion.

CHOOSE TEXTS

For this question, like others about developing ideas, you'll want a text where students need to make an inference. Poems can be useful for drawing conclusions because they frequently call for abstract thinking, yet their brevity keeps students from becoming too frustrated. Also remember to use informational selections. Recognizing the implications of a real-world problem enhances critical thinking.

The following tools will help you answer Question 2.6.

PROVIDE PRACTICE USING TOOLS IN CHAPTER 5
- Anchor Chart 1: Finding Surprising or Helpful Details in a Story or Poem
- Anchor Chart 2: Finding Surprising or Helpful Details in an Informational Text
- Anchor Chart 3: Explaining Importance in Fiction and Nonfiction

What character trait (or feeling) does [character] mainly show in this story?

EXPLAIN THE CONCEPT: CHARACTER TRAITS AND FEELINGS

Remember that character *traits* and character *feelings* are not the same thing. While a character's feelings may change several times throughout a story, and there may be many feelings, it's different for traits. In traditional stories like fables and fairy tales, the character usually has one main trait that is the source of their success or downfall. The character may be brave, honest, foolish, greedy, or something else. In other texts where characters are more complex, a few traits may be present, and sometimes a trait may change over the course of the story. Greed may turn into generosity; fear may evolve into bravery. Still, there will likely be fewer traits than feelings. A character with a negative trait is more likely to change, often showing a more positive trait at the end of a story.

To decide what trait or feeling a character shows, look carefully at how a character *reacts* to problems. Then decide whether the reaction is positive or negative. Next, consider the positive and negative trait (or feeling) and refine your choice by selecting a more precise word if needed (a shade of meaning—like *elated* instead of *happy*).

CHOOSE TEXTS

This is the most basic question we can ask about characters and will be most useful with younger students. (Older students should be tasked with some of the more complex character questions.) Good sources for identifying character traits are selections like fables or biographies where the trait is directly related to the outcome of the story. For character feelings (which abound in most stories), be sure the character's feeling contributes to their behavior or an important decision. You may also want to choose sources that focus on a specific feeling like hope or joy.

The following tools provide practice with concepts important for answering Question 3.1.

PROVIDE PRACTICE USING TOOLS IN CHAPTER 5

- Anchor Chart 5: Positive Character Traits and Shades of Meaning
- Anchor Chart 6: Negative Character Traits and Shades of Meaning
- Anchor Chart 7: Positive Character Feelings and Shades of Meaning
- Anchor Chart 8: Negative Character Feelings and Shades of Meaning
- Anchor Chart 3: Explaining Importance in Fiction and Nonfiction

What is the character's attitude, and how does it make a difference?

EXPLAIN THE CONCEPT: CHARACTER ATTITUDES

When we say that someone has a "good attitude" or a "bad attitude," we mean that they see life at that moment in more of a positive way or a negative way. Attitude is important because a positive attitude typically helps people feel happier about their lives, while always seeing the downside of situations leads to feelings of discontent. If we look more closely, we can be more specific about positive and negative attitudes—which helps us better understand why people (and characters) behave as they do. Keep in mind that attitude is important because it makes a difference to the way a character responds to a problem and makes decisions. A character's (or person's) attitude might change based on how other people treat them. For example, maybe a bully has a bad attitude because someone has bullied her. Always try to figure out the *reason* for someone's attitude.

Note that these same attitude words (and just about any adjective) can be used to describe the *tone* of a piece of writing. Tone means how the author or narrator *feels* about the topic. The words an author chooses to describe something are the best key to tone.

CHOOSE TEXTS

It may be easier for students to recognize character attitude when the attitude is negative. Choose sources where students can see the impact of attitude on the outcome of a story or the way characters respond to each other. Consider using stories with a first person narrator as the attitude will be especially visible. Help students distinguish between attitudes and traits. Attitudes account for in-the-moment behavior (like resentment of a younger sibling for getting a special favor from Mom) whereas a trait governs behavior in general. Perhaps the person is typically honest, hardworking, or timid. Always help students determine *why* the character demonstrates a particular attitude.

The following tools provide practice for answering Question 3.2.

PROVIDE PRACTICE USING TOOLS IN CHAPTER 5

- Anchor Chart 9: Positive Character Attitudes and Author's Tone
- Anchor Chart 10: Negative Character Attitudes and Author's Tone

What motivated [character] to _____?

EXPLAIN THE CONCEPT: CHARACTER MOTIVATION

When we ask what motivates a character or person, we are trying to find out the reason for their behavior or actions. People are motivated by different things. They might be motivated by a basic need, something they desire for themselves or others, or a strong feeling or value that guides their life. Sometimes a character can be motivated by one thing at the beginning of a story, and something else later. For instance, a greedy person may become generous. You can often tell what motivates a character early in the story, though sometimes it takes a while to see it clearly. Think about the fable "The Tortoise and the Hare." At the beginning of that story, the hare appears motivated by the desire to win. But at the end of the tale, we see that his true motivation was to succeed with little effort.

When you're trying to figure out what motivates someone, first decide which of these three areas is the best fit (basic need, want, or value). Then within the area you chose, find a more specific label. Always try to explain how motivation is important in the text, too.

CHOOSE TEXTS

When choosing a text for character motivation, make sure to look for a character who has a clear goal and pursues it with determination. Along the way, the author will illuminate _why_ the goal is so important to the character, which is the _motivation_. In many books, there will be hurdles to overcome, which will make the motivation even clearer to readers.

The following tools provide practice with concepts important for answering Question 3.3.

PROVIDE PRACTICE USING TOOLS IN CHAPTER 5

Anchor Chart 11: Analyzing Character Motivations
Anchor Chart 3: Explaining Importance in Fiction and Nonfiction

What is the relationship between [Character A] and [Character B]?

EXPLAIN THE CONCEPT: CHARACTER RELATIONSHIPS

People connect with each other for different reasons. They probably either need or enjoy each other, although the reason for the need or enjoyment will vary depending on the situation or the people involved. Regardless of the kind of relationship, it will likely change the participants in some way. It could make their life better and happier. Or it could make their life more challenging and difficult.

Sometimes characters who are connected to each other have positive, healthy relationships because they both value honesty, kindness, and other positive qualities. But other times the relationship is a negative one because one of the characters (or maybe both) behaves badly. For instance, when one person is a bully, and another is the victim, this is an unhealthy relationship. The bully is using their power to make the other person feel powerless. Although more than one word could apply to the two characters you are analyzing, choose the one word you think is the *best* fit.

CHOOSE TEXTS

Texts for analyzing character relationships call for sources where at least one of the characters has a clear point of view about what is important to them. For this question, the characters will likely be dependent on each other in some way. Readers will need to determine exactly *how* they are connected and whether the relationship is healthy or unhealthy.

The following tools provide practice with concepts important for answering Question 3.4.

PROVIDE PRACTICE USING TOOLS IN CHAPTER 5

- Anchor Chart 12: Analyzing Character Relationships
- Anchor Chart 3: Explaining Importance in Fiction and Nonfiction

What is [Character's/Author's] point of view about _____? How does the character (or author) show this?

EXPLAIN THE CONCEPT: CHARACTER'S OR AUTHOR'S POINT OF VIEW

When a question asks about a character's or author's point of view, it is not inquiring as to whether the story is told (or the information is provided) by a first, second, or third person narrator. It is not even asking what the character or author had a point of view *about*, as that information will be included in the question. Instead, your job is to figure out what the character (or author) believes to be true about something: Is the character for something or against it, liking it or disliking it? The challenge will be to choose the most helpful evidence to *show* the character's or author's viewpoint. You will know you have the best evidence if you can explain *why* it is important.

CHOOSE TEXTS

When choosing texts that highlight a character's (or author's) point of view, choose a source where the character is complex and the character (or author) is passionate about something. This might be a good opportunity to choose a biographical piece, an essay, or speech of a person who cares deeply about a personal, community, or global goal. You could also choose a poem where the author conveys the strong emotions that accompany strong beliefs.

The following tools provide practice with concepts important for answering Question 3.5.

PROVIDE PRACTICE USING TOOLS IN CHAPTER 5

- Anchor Chart 13: Reasons for a Character's Behavior
- Anchor Chart 3: Explaining Importance in Fiction and Nonfiction

What are the most important differences between [Character A] and [Character B]?

EXPLAIN THE CONCEPT: CHARACTER DIFFERENCES

When you look for important differences between characters, see beyond their gender or appearance. Instead, think about each character's goals, motivation, and attitude. Also think about the character's life circumstances: Do they come from a background where they've been respected and nurtured? Or have they been the victim of racism or other unfair treatment? How has their past made a difference in their current thinking and actions? In other words, think beyond their point of view to understand *why* they think this way, and *how* this is important to the story.

CHOOSE TEXTS

This is another question that calls for sources with two dynamic characters. The characters may have similar goals with different motivations or means of achieving them, or perhaps they are aiming for different goals. They could be different in other ways, too. Look for the biggest differences at the beginning of the story. By the end, the characters may have resolved their differences. At least one of the characters in the story will probably change.

The following tools provide practice with concepts important for answering Question 3.6.

PROVIDE PRACTICE USING TOOLS IN CHAPTER 5

- Anchor Chart 13: Reasons for a Character's Behavior
- Anchor Chart 14: Comparing Characters

What is the relationship between [the setting] and [the problem] in _____?

EXPLAIN THE CONCEPT:
RELATIONSHIP BETWEEN TEXT ELEMENTS

This question is fun to think about because it can involve your imagination along with understanding the information in the text. The most important thing to keep in mind when answering a question about the connection between text elements is that one element of a story (the characters, setting, problem, events, or solution) affects every other element. Sometimes the easiest way to see this is if you change one of the story elements (like setting). Now, consider how a different time or place would make a difference to the problem or how it got solved (among other possible differences).

Setting

A good way to explore setting is to read stories, real or fictional, set in the past or set in a different part of our country or world, because it's easier to see how setting matters when it is not the time and place in which _we_ live. We might, however, take a story set in our part of the world right now and imagine how it would be different if it took place fifty years ago, a hundred years ago, in a warmer or colder climate, in a part of the world where women are less respected—or so many other conditions of time and place.

Problem

Before you can understand how the problem in a story is connected to another text element, you need a good understanding of the problem itself. Sometimes finding the problem in a story is simple. The author explains it right at the beginning and throughout the rest of the story, shows how the problem gets worse at first, and then gets solved. There are often a few attempts to solve the problem before there is a solution. If it's the _real_ problem in the story, it will connect directly to the solution.

But sometimes it's easy to miss the real problem in a story because the situation doesn't look like a big issue when it is introduced. One example would be Little Red Riding Hood, when she talks to the wolf on the way to her granny's house. You know you shouldn't talk to strangers. But nothing horrible happens right away. Later in the story the wolf finds his way to Granny's house and tries to eat her. This may lead readers to conclude that the problem was the wolf's attempt to eat the grandmother. Of course, this *is* a problem, but it's not how the problem began. What *drives* the events in this story? That's what you're looking for to identify the problem.

Another tricky situation with story problems is that the problem may have gotten started before the story even began. For instance, in a book about Martin Luther King Jr., the problem may be discrimination based on skin color. But this didn't begin on the first page of the story. This began many years ago, and the story shows the effects of the problem and King's response to it. Always try to trace the events of the story back to their true beginning.

Another word you might see instead of *problem* is *conflict*—which means about the same thing. In fact, you might be asked about the *kind* of conflict in the story. It could be a personal conflict. Perhaps the character can't swim and is afraid to go to camp where he'll be expected to swim every day. It could be a conflict with another person, like the character having an argument with her best friend. Or it could be a conflict with nature. A character goes on a long hike and encounters an avalanche.

CHOOSE TEXTS

This question can be asked about the connection between any story parts, but I like to include a focus on setting because setting sometimes gets overlooked when we talk about text elements. What if the setting had been different? Would the situation have been resolved in the same way if it occurred at another time in history or elsewhere in the world? What if it happened right now, today? To get started, look for fiction or non-fiction stories set in a specific historical period—perhaps slavery in America, immigration, civil rights in the era of Martin Luther King Jr., treatment of Native Americans. The list goes on.

The following tools provide practice with concepts important for answering Question 3.7.

PROVIDE PRACTICE USING TOOLS IN CHAPTER 5

- Anchor Chart 15: How Setting Matters in a Story or Real-Life Event
- Anchor Chart 16: Analyzing the Problem
- Anchor Chart 3: Explaining Importance in Fiction and Nonfiction

What does [word] mean and what clue in the text helped you to understand it?

EXPLAIN THE CONCEPT: DETERMINING WORD MEANING

Any time you see a question that asks about a word's meaning, know that you can find a clue to this meaning somewhere in the passage, probably very close to the "mystery" word. *Always* look for the clue. Some common kinds of clues include a definition, synonym, antonym, or example. Let's suppose the word is *rambunctious*:

- The children were very *rambunctious* when they went out for recess, racing all over the playground and screaming loudly. (*Racing all over the playground and screaming loudly* is an **example** of *rambunctious* behavior.)
- "Don't be so *rambunctious*," the teacher scolded. "I don't like unruly behavior." (*Unruly* is a **synonym** for *rambunctious*. The words mean about the same thing.)
- Some of the children were *rambunctious* as they stood in line, but others waited calmly. (*Calmly* is an **antonym**.)
- The children were full of energy and difficult to control. They certainly were *rambunctious* today. (*Full of energy and difficult to control* is a good **definition** of *rambunctious*.)

CHOOSE TEXTS

Something important to keep in mind when choosing words for students to identify meaning is that there *must* be a clue provided somewhere within the text. This sounds simple enough, but you'll be surprised how many words you find that would be great for vocabulary focus where the text does *not* offer a context clue. This doesn't mean you can't teach the word. But it's not a good assessment question. On new standards-based assessments, there are many words whose meanings students are asked to identify, and every one of them will include a context clue. They will mostly be two-part questions. Part A will ask the word's meaning. Part B will ask for the clue that led students to their understanding.

PROVIDE PRACTICE USING TOOLS IN CHAPTER 5

These examples for determining word meaning should be sufficient for Question 4.1, with no Anchor Charts needed.

What word might the author use to make the meaning in this [sentence] clearer?

EXPLAIN THE CONCEPT: CHOOSING PRECISE WORDS

The point of using "clear" language is to use as few words as possible to say what you mean. "Clearer" language is *precise* language. So, when a question asks about words that would make meaning clearer, think about words that would give you a sharper picture in your mind. It could be a proper or specific noun instead of a general noun. It could be a strong verb instead of a weaker one. Sometimes an adjective or adverb can make your meaning clearer, but other times these words detract from meaning by taking the focus away from the important word. Whenever you can, avoid words like *really* and *very*. For example, it's better to say, "He was brave," not "He was very brave." *Very* gets in the way of the key word, *brave*. Here are some other examples that show *precise* words:

- That is a beautiful *poodle*—instead of That is a beautiful *dog*.
- "I want a popsicle," Jack *whined*—instead of "I want a popsicle," Jack *said*.
- I feel *frustrated*—instead of I feel *sad*.
- Lily *sprinted* down the street—instead of Lily *ran* down the street.

One additional point to keep in mind when choosing more precise language is that the word you select should maintain the same tone as the rest of the writing. For instance, if the author says, "Maria *smiled* when she won the race." You might say instead, "Maria *beamed* when she won the race." But you probably wouldn't say, "Maria *smirked* when she won the race," because a smirk is not a kind way to smile and this wouldn't fit the mood in the rest of the story.

CHOOSE TEXTS

If you teach with well-crafted text, the language is probably already clear. Instead, use samples of student writing (names removed). Or you can write your own paragraph with places where students can spot the need for more precise language. Or you can use the short paragraphs I wrote and included for this question in Chapter 7: Sample

Constructed Responses. Asking students to choose new words for both paragraphs would demonstrate the importance of selecting language that conveys the appropriate tone.

PROVIDE PRACTICE USING TOOLS IN CHAPTER 5

These examples for choosing precise words should be sufficient for Question 4.2, with no Anchor Charts needed.

What words create the tone in this [paragraph]? What is the tone?

EXPLAIN THE CONCEPT: AUTHOR'S TONE

Readers often get confused by these three words: tone, mood, and voice. Maybe this explanation will help. *Tone* is how the author feels about the topic. *Mood* is how you feel when you read the author's words. *Voice* is the personality of the author, which you can see in the writing. Here, we're focusing on tone.

One way to think about tone is to decide if it is formal or informal. A formal tone would make the writing sound like you're writing an official letter. An informal tone sounds more like you're communicating with a friend. Text messages usually have a very informal tone. But that's not all you should consider when thinking about tone. Almost any adjective could describe the tone and sometimes there will be more than one tone in a text. A few might be: serious, cheerful, sad, hopeful, anxious. The same words that might describe a character can also be used to describe an author's tone.

The best way to identify tone is to look at what the author chooses to focus on and the words the author uses to describe a setting, characters (or real people), and events. For example, describing rain as a "gentle shower" creates a different tone than calling it a "raging downpour."

CHOOSE TEXTS

Both fiction and nonfiction will work for teaching tone. For older students, look at the tone of editorials or news articles. It's always a moment of enlightenment when students realize there is no such thing as "objective" text, that everything we read has a slant to it, subtle though it might be. Excerpts from classic literature are also great for teaching tone as they will encourage students to look beyond the content of the story or poem to examine the language more deeply. Whatever you choose, make sure there are at least two examples students can find that convey the same tone.

The following tools provide practice for answering Question 4.3.

PROVIDE PRACTICE USING TOOLS IN CHAPTER 5

- Anchor Chart 9: Positive Character Attitudes and Author's Tone
- Anchor Chart 10: Negative Character Attitudes and Author's Tone

What author's craft (like description, dialogue, internal dialogue, and gesture) does the author use in this [part of the story] and why do you think the author included it?

EXPLAIN THE CONCEPT: LITERARY TECHNIQUES

Author's crafts (also called literary techniques) are strategies authors use to make their writing more interesting and fun to read. When you read a story you love, it might seem unimaginable that you could write something that amazing. And maybe your writing won't look like that by tomorrow. But here's the real deal: Authors know a few basic tricks that make writing sound great, and when you know these tricks, too, your writing will be better than you ever thought it could be.

The first step in becoming a good writer yourself is to recognize these crafts in stories you read. They've been there all along, but you didn't know to look for them. Once you know what to look for, you'll spot them easily. We will focus on four crafts: description, dialogue, internal dialogue, and gesture. Remember that even a short part of a text can include several crafts.

CHOOSE TEXTS

Almost any story you would want to read aloud to your students or that you would encourage students to read independently would demonstrate the use of many literary techniques (or crafts). Be aware, however, that a book or author may feature some crafts over others. So, if you want to focus on how authors use dialogue effectively, choose a story that contains a lot of conversation. Or for a focus on internal dialogue, look for stories with a first person narrator, because that character's inner thoughts will frequently be revealed. Your question about author's craft can ask students to identify a single literary technique or multiple literary techniques.

The following tool provides practice for answering Question 4.4.

PROVIDE PRACTICE USING TOOLS IN CHAPTER 5

- Anchor Chart 18: Analyzing Author's Craft in Narrative Text

What figurative language (like simile, metaphor, personification, idiom, or hyperbole) does the author use in this [paragraph] and why do you think the author chose it?

EXPLAIN THE CONCEPT: FIGURATIVE LANGUAGE

There are different kinds of figurative language that authors use to make ideas stand out and to create more vivid pictures in readers' minds. It's called "figurative" language because the words don't always mean exactly what they say. However, the meaning still needs to make sense. For example, you could use the simile *as red as an apple* because an apple is usually red. But you wouldn't say *as red as a shirt* because a shirt could be many different colors. Similarly, you could use the metaphor *the snow was a blanket* because when snow covers something it does seem like a blanket. You would not say *The car is a blanket* because a car doesn't act as a cover. You will often find figurative language in poetry and stories. You will find figurative language (particularly similes) in informational text, too, especially when a comparison will help you better understand a new concept. Finally, remember that an author can use more than one kind of figurative language in a piece of writing.

CHOOSE TEXTS

Poets use lots of figurative language because one of the goals of a poem is to paint vivid pictures in the reader's mind. But you'll find figurative language in other writing, too. Some authors of both fiction and nonfiction write in a way that sounds more like poetry than prose. And it's often the figurative language that makes the writing poetic. Some authors I love who use figurative language well are Cynthia Rylant, Robert Burleigh, and Nicola Davies. The latter two authors write a lot of narrative nonfiction. I love to show students that informational text can also include beautiful language.

The following tool provides practice for answering Question 4.5.

PROVIDE PRACTICE USING TOOLS IN CHAPTER 5

- Anchor Chart 19: Analyzing Figurative Language

What elements of a [fable] did you find in this text? Find at least two elements and explain how the author uses them.

EXPLAIN THE CONCEPT: GENRE ELEMENTS: FABLE

A fable is a very short story that teaches a lesson. The characters are often animals, although they talk and behave like people. (When animals talk, it is called anthropomorphism, not personification.) Fables are called *traditional* literature because the stories have been told for hundreds of years. Have you heard of Aesop? Aesop was from Greece and is credited with creating these stories—although no one knows for sure. There are modern fables, too. Any story with a moral that can be applied to life outside the story itself might be considered a fable. An example of a modern fable, a short story with a moral, is *The Giving Tree* by Shel Silverstein.

CHOOSE TEXTS

If you don't have easy access to a book of fables, check *Aesop's Fables* on Project Gutenberg (gutenberg.org). This is an archive of out-of-copyright sources that you may download for free (also free of guilt). Beyond that, consider other more modern stories that are also considered fables. These might include *The Polar Express* and *Just a Dream* by Chris Van Allsburg, and *The Lorax* and *Yertle the Turtle* by Dr. Seuss. For older students, there's *Animal Farm* by George Orwell.

The following tool provides practice with concepts important for answering Question 4.6.

PROVIDE PRACTICE USING TOOLS IN CHAPTER 5

· Anchor Chart 20: Analyzing a Fable

Why do you think the author wrote this as a [poem]?

EXPLAIN THE CONCEPT: GENRE ELEMENTS: POEM

An author can choose from many different genres, but here we will think about why an author might want to write something in the form of a poem. Poetry is a good choice (instead of a story, news article, etc.) if you have really strong feelings about your topic and it lends itself to language that conveys emotions and complex images—presented in a poetic format. What do we mean by the "language and format" of a poem? The Anchor Chart for poetry will give you all the details you need to better understand a poem. But in general, first think about the look and sound of a poem when you read it aloud. Then focus on the language the poet uses to express ideas. Finally, once you have a good understanding of the meaning, consider the poet's intent (or purpose) in writing the poem.

CHOOSE TEXTS

When choosing texts for understanding any genre, make sure they exemplify multiple characteristics of the genre. Moreover, when you want to help students recognize why an author would select a specific genre, also make sure that the topic of the text is a good fit for that genre. For example, likely topics for poetry to which children can relate might include things like nature, family, and famous people from history—among others. Be sure to include works of classic poetry like those by Robert Frost, Langston Hughes, and Robert Louis Stevenson. "Fun" poems by authors such as Shel Silverstein and Jack Prelutsky should not be the only poetry younger students experience.

The following tool provides practice with concepts important for answering Question 4.7.

PROVIDE PRACTICE USING TOOLS IN CHAPTER 5

- Anchor Chart 21: Analyzing a Poem

What is this text feature and what is the most likely reason the author included it?

EXPLAIN THE CONCEPT: TEXT FEATURES

When we talk about text features, we're referring to the visuals an author adds to an informational text that are not part of the main content. There are lots of text features to learn about, and before you can answer this question, you need to know their names and how to recognize them. Text features include things like glossaries, graphs, maps, bullet points, and bolded words, and are found mostly in informational writing. Authors include them because information can be complicated and text features make important points stand out so readers can see and understand them more easily.

Sometimes the feature *clarifies* meaning the author has provided within the text. An example of this might be a timeline that shows a sequence of events that the author took many paragraphs to describe. Seeing this graphic adds perspective for readers who benefit from visual cues, not just words. Other times, the text feature *adds* meaning that is not part of the main content. For instance, there might be a text box that provides additional details about the topic for readers who want to learn more about it.

Your job as a reader is first to understand the information the author is providing with the text feature, and then to decide why the author wanted to include it. How is it contributing to your understanding?

CHOOSE TEXTS

Beyond the obvious need to choose informational sources that include text features, try to give students opportunities to explore things that go beyond glossaries, headings, italicized words, and other widespread features. Instead, highlight less common ones such as cut aways and text boxes. More importantly, choose features that are sometimes included for clarification and other times add content and new knowledge.

The following tool provides practice for answering Question 5.1.

PROVIDE PRACTICE USING TOOLS IN CHAPTER 5

- Anchor Chart 22: Analyzing Informational Text Features

What text structure did the author choose for writing [about this topic] and what is the most likely reason the author chose it?

EXPLAIN THE CONCEPT: TEXT STRUCTURES

Text structure means how a text is organized, how the author presents information. In nonfiction there are just a few main organizational patterns (or structures). These include:

- Descriptive (with main ideas and details)
- Compare/Contrast
- Cause and Effect
- Problem/Solution
- Sequence of Events (or steps)
- Narrative Nonfiction

Authors think hard about how they organize their writing because a good structure helps readers' comprehension. Always try to identify the structure, because once you've figured it out, it will help you understand the content of the piece better.

One thing that might be confusing about text structure is that there is often more than one structure in an informational book or article. You might find a compare/contrast structure in one place and a problem/solution structure a few paragraphs later. When you see a question about text structure, the question will tell you whether you need to look at the whole source, or just a part of it.

Either way, think about *why* the author chose that structure.

CHOOSE TEXTS

When we teach with informational text, our go-to sources are often descriptive with main ideas and details because they provide access to all those text features we want students to explore (headings, bolded words, glossaries, and more). Yes, we should use descriptive text often. But let's broaden our reach and be more intentional about incorporating other informational structures, too. I especially like short pieces that address two sides of an issue because they're great for comparing and contrasting and invite students' critical thinking. I also like narrative nonfiction where the author provides information in story form (for example: a sea turtle whose life you follow from hatchling, through the perils of survival, to the moment decades later when she lays the eggs that will become the next generation). Stories with embedded facts are a great way to build knowledge *and* interest around a topic.

The following tool provides practice with concepts important for answering Question 5.2.

PROVIDE PRACTICE USING TOOLS IN CHAPTER 5

• Anchor Chart 23: Analyzing Informational Text Structures

What kind of information does the author provide in [paragraph A] and why does the author include it?

EXPLAIN THE CONCEPT: KIND OF INFORMATION IN A PASSAGE

To determine the kind of information an author includes in a paragraph or other specific part of a text, first decide whether the text is literary or informational. Remember that different types of text include different elements. If the source is narrative (a true or fictional story) the information will probably be about the characters, setting, a problem, events that occur within the story, the resolution, the ending, or the central idea or lesson the story teaches. If the source is nonfiction with a descriptive format, expect information such as main ideas, topics, subtopics, facts, opinions, introductions, conclusions, comparisons, causes, and effects.

The most important guideline to keep in mind for a question that asks for the *kind* of information the author includes is that this is a question about *structure*, not about *content*. For example, you might explain that the author is providing information about the relationship between characters. You don't need to describe the relationship itself (loving, loyal, or something else).

CHOOSE TEXTS

This is a question that begs for both literary and informational sources because the kinds of information the author provides will vary depending on the text type. For students who are new to the structural analysis of a text, choose an element that is obvious, like introducing the problem or learning about the setting. For more advanced readers, focus on something more nuanced, like the relationship between characters in a story, or the statement of an opinion rather than a fact in an informational article.

The following tool provides practice for answering Question 5.3.

PROVIDE PRACTICE USING TOOLS IN CHAPTER 5

- Anchor Chart 24: Analyzing the Kind of Information an Author Includes in a [Paragraph]

How does [paragraph A] connect to [paragraph B]?

EXPLAIN THE CONCEPT: CONNECTION BETWEEN [PARAGRAPHS]

Any story, article, poem, or other text that you read is like a puzzle: The parts fit together in just the right way so that everything makes sense. It's easy to overlook how the text is organized when you are reading for enjoyment or even when you are reading for information. You're just trying to get the meaning. But here's a hint that might be helpful: If you pay attention to the way the author has organized the writing, you'll understand what you're reading even better. Try to recognize the kind of information that each paragraph or part of the text contains. Then check to see how the information in one part of the text connects to the part before or after it.

Think especially about parts that are right next to each other. There are lots of ways the parts can fit together. One common one is the next paragraph (or stanza) gives more details or an example of an idea that the author explained in the previous paragraph. Maybe the first paragraph is about dogs' sense of smell and the paragraph that follows gives an example that shows the power of the nose. Or it could be that the author introduces a whole new idea in the next paragraph. Following the paragraph on dogs' sense of smell, the next paragraph could describe their sight.

CHOOSE TEXTS

Both fiction and nonfiction are appropriate for asking this question. But make sure you choose a text that is well-written and logically organized. Also, try to answer the question yourself before asking students to do so. If *you* can't see how two paragraphs (stanzas, or other short passages) fit together, your students won't be able to recognize the connection either. Don't overlook poetry when asking this question. Choose poems with short stanzas (perhaps four lines per stanza) so the content isn't overwhelming. Regardless of the text you choose, modeling the process of how *you* determine connections between parts of a text will make this task more manageable for students.

The following tool provides practice for answering Question 5.4.

PROVIDE PRACTICE USING TOOLS IN CHAPTER 5

- Anchor Chart 25: Analyzing How Parts of a Text Fit Together

Why did the author choose to begin/ end the story with this [paragraph]?

EXPLAIN THE CONCEPT: BEGINNING AND ENDING OF A STORY

Authors work hard on the beginning and ending of their stories because they know how important these parts are to readers. If the beginning catches your interest, you will probably keep reading. If it's confusing or boring, you might put the story down and choose another one. It should set the tone and give you a little information about what will come next. This could relate to the characters, the problem, or the action. Endings are important because you want to feel satisfied that the story has been worth your time now that all the action is over. This doesn't mean you always want a *happy* ending, but you do want to feel that all the loose ends are tied up—for both the characters and for you.

What kinds of beginnings and endings might an author write? There are many ways to craft a beginning or ending. Also decide whether you think the beginning or ending you've read is a good one. When a question asks about beginnings or endings, it will probably tell you exactly how many paragraphs or lines to consider. Note too that a beginning or ending could be written with more than one purpose in mind.

CHOOSE TEXTS

When asking this question, choose literature where story beginnings and endings are effective and well-written. Picture books are good options because the "beginning" is often the first page; the "ending" is the final page. Familiar chapter books will work too, because students can evaluate the effectiveness of the beginning or ending based on content they've already read. Whatever sources you choose, try to select beginnings and endings that have been crafted differently based on the strategies identified in the anchor charts for beginnings and endings.

The following tools provide practice for answering Question 5.5.

PROVIDE PRACTICE USING TOOLS IN CHAPTER 5

- Anchor Chart 26: Analyzing How an Author Begins a Story
- Anchor Chart 27: Analyzing How an Author Ends a Story

Where is the flashback in this story and why did the author most likely include it?

EXPLAIN THE CONCEPT: FLASHBACK THAT PROVIDES BACKGROUND

When authors are concerned that readers may not have enough understanding of a topic to comprehend the story or informational piece, they find a way to provide that information within the text to build the necessary background. There are several strategies authors can use for this. One way they can build background in fictional stories or narrative nonfiction is through a flashback, which is a memory. The author interrupts the action with a scene where the character thinks back to something that happened before the current point of the story.

A character facing a challenge now might think back to a time when he experienced a similar feeling, or when she encountered a comparable problem. For example, if the story is about a girl who is afraid of a dog, there might be a flashback to a time before this story was told when the girl was bitten by a dog. This often provides insight into how a character will probably respond to the current situation.

CHOOSE TEXTS

Flashback is a good place to begin to understand how an author provides background information. For asking questions about flashback, choose stories with well-developed, robust characters (or real people) who face personal challenges. Look for the flashback to shed light on how a character's past challenges impact the challenge they are facing now.

The following tools provide practice with concepts important for answering Question 5.6.

PROVIDE PRACTICE USING TOOLS IN CHAPTER 5

- Anchor Chart 28: Analyzing a Flashback
- Anchor Chart 3: Explaining Importance in Fiction and Nonfiction

What is the backstory for this [story], and why did the author most likely include it?

EXPLAIN THE CONCEPT: BACKSTORY THAT PROVIDES CONTEXT

Unlike a flashback—which is in the middle of a text—a backstory is usually at the beginning of a story, before the author introduces the problem. In some stories, the author wants you to know what life was like before the current situation occurred. Life might have been better then, or it could have been more challenging. Authors provide this information because they think it will help you appreciate what's happening now more thoroughly. Sometimes a backstory seems confusing because you're not sure how it fits into what happens next. Be patient and keep reading. You'll see how everything connects when the author introduces the problem.

If you are reading a news article, the author may include the backstory at the end of the piece. Although this sounds strange (writing the events that occurred beforehand at the end), there is a good reason for this. Authors want to get your attention, and so begin with the breaking news. They assume you've kept up with the topic by reading previous articles or watching television news. But in case you've forgotten some of the details, they catch you up with the background after explaining the most recent developments.

CHOOSE TEXTS

To teach backstory, look for stories where the problem is not introduced right away. For example, if the current problem is about two girls who used to be best friends, but no longer speak to each other, the story may begin with a description of the fun things they did together in the past—to provide a contrast to their relationship now. When focusing on informational articles, choose accounts that are updates on a topic that has been discussed previously. This gives the author a reason to summarize key points from the earlier pieces in a "backstory." In this case, look for the backstory at the end of the text, not the beginning.

The following tools provide practice for answering Question 5.7.

PROVIDE PRACTICE USING TOOLS IN CHAPTER 5

- Anchor Chart 29: Analyzing a Backstory
- Anchor Chart 3: Explaining Importance in Fiction and Nonfiction

Why do you think the author included this quote from another author at the beginning of this [chapter]?

EXPLAIN THE CONCEPT: QUOTE THAT BEGINS A [CHAPTER]

Sometimes there's a quote from a different author at the beginning of a chapter or book. In our haste to get to the "meat" of the text we may race past these words with barely a glance. But these quotes (which also have a fancy name: epigraphs) deserve more attention. They are a kind of foreshadowing, a clue to something important about the book or chapter. This importance often relates to a central idea, though it could also lead to insights about a character, a setting, or something else.

CHOOSE TEXTS

Look for these quotes mostly in stories, at the beginning of a book or chapter, though the stories could be fiction or nonfiction (or perhaps a biography). When the book is a picture book, you'll probably find the quote on a page before the story begins. If the quote is at the beginning of a chapter, the chapter may only be numbered, with no title. Instead of using the chapter title to hint at what's to come, those clues are hidden in the quote.

The following tools provide practice with concepts important for answering Question 5.8.

PROVIDE PRACTICE USING TOOLS IN CHAPTER 5

- Anchor Chart 30: Analyzing a Quote from Another Author at the Beginning of a Book or Chapter
- Anchor Chart 3: Explaining Importance in Fiction and Nonfiction

How would this story change if it were told from [new narrator's] point of view?

EXPLAIN THE CONCEPT: DIFFERENT POINT OF VIEW

Answering this question will help you with your writing as well as your reading because sometimes you will be asked to write a story from a different character's point of view. For that, it will be important to understand how a story changes based on who is telling it. You do *not* need to rewrite the story from a different point of view when you answer this question. You only need to notice the details in the story that let you know what motivates the character, their attitude, and their feelings.

Although *this* question won't require rewriting the story, rewriting a story from a different character's point of view is also a viable task. If you *do* need to rewrite the story sometime, you can use what you know about the new narrator to tell a great story. For rewriting, remember that the events of the story will still be the same. The only thing that will change is what the character *thinks* about these events (showing the motivation, attitude, and feelings). In your story, include some description, dialogue, gestures, and "inside" thoughts in the character's head to show the new narrator's point of view.

CHOOSE TEXTS

This question works especially well when the story is written in the first person because the current narrator's point of view is clear. There needs to be a second strong character as well who thinks differently from the first narrator. Students like it when the character from whose perspective they will write is a child about their age. This makes the voice easier for them to imagine. Because it is sometimes difficult to find appropriate first person narratives, it is also possible to use a text with a third person narrator (not one of the characters in the story) and consider how the story would change if it was retold from the perspective of one of the characters themselves. Again, be sure to choose a character with a clear point of view.

The following tools provide practice with concepts important for answering Question 6.1.

PROVIDE PRACTICE USING TOOLS IN CHAPTER 5

- Anchor Chart 7: Positive Character Feelings and Shades of Meaning
- Anchor Chart 8: Negative Character Feelings and Shades of Meaning
- Anchor Chart 9: Positive Character Attitudes and Author's Tone
- Anchor Chart 10: Negative Character Attitudes and Author's Tone
- Anchor Chart 11: Analyzing Character Motivations

What is your point of view about _____, and how is it the same or different from the point of view of the author?

EXPLAIN THE CONCEPT: READER'S POINT OF VIEW

This is a great question to consider for informational text, especially when the topic is controversial, leading to different points of view. Some examples would be whether school uniforms are a good idea, the value of zoos, allowing cell phones in school, the advantages and disadvantages of distance learning, and many other issues important to our community or our world. While you may have had lots of experience "defending your point of view" (commonly known as arguing) with parents or siblings, there are a few more "rules" when you argue in writing and want to convince someone that your point of view is the best point of view.

For a constructed response, you can't just announce your opinion and expect everyone to believe you. You need reasons and evidence. For the best arguments you also need to follow some logical steps, so that your point of view is convincing. Present your reasons and evidence in an order that will make sense to other people. Begin with your strongest reason first because that will be the best way to get your opponents' attention. Do not begin by telling your opponent why they are wrong, because that will just make them angrier. But, once you've (calmly) explained all your best reasons—with evidence—*then* show why the opposing position is not as strong. This same approach works when you are "arguing in writing": constructing an answer to a point of view question.

CHOOSE TEXTS

For the best results with this question you will need two articles on a topic, each representing a different point of view. It's easier for students to determine their own viewpoint when they can examine the topic from more than one perspective. That said, providing too much information might be overwhelming, I have found that Read-Works, easily accessed free of charge at www.readworks.org, offers the perfect solution. Search "News Debate" and at your fingertips: a long list of options at various reading levels that offer two sides of an issue within the same brief article. Even these short-ish pieces can lead to long answers because of all the steps involved. Consider saving this question for students who are ready for the kind of logical reasoning necessary for quality persuasive writing.

The following tools provide practice with concepts important for answering Question 6.2.

PROVIDE PRACTICE USING TOOLS IN CHAPTER 5

- Checklist 2: Defending a Point of View
- Anchor Chart 2: Finding Surprising or Helpful Details in an Informational Text
- Anchor Chart 3: Explaining Importance in Fiction and Nonfiction

What was the author's purpose for including this [paragraph/sentence]?

EXPLAIN THE CONCEPT:
AUTHOR'S REASON FOR INCLUDING PARTICULAR INFORMATION

Most of the author's purpose questions you see matched to new standards will be different from what you've seen in the past. Not so long ago, purpose questions related to a *full* text, and the question might have asked, "What was the author's purpose for writing this article about sharks?" You would have likely answered, "The author wrote this article to *inform* me about different kinds of sharks and why some sharks can be dangerous to humans." If the text had been a story, you would have said that the purpose was "to *entertain.*" If it was a news debate, you would have identified the author's purpose as "to *persuade.*"

Questions like these didn't lead to very deep thinking, but with new standards, that has changed. Now, questions about author's purpose typically inquire about a *part* of a text. For example, "Why did the author place this sentence first in this paragraph?" "Why do you think the author added this paragraph before moving to a new topic?" The reasons for including a paragraph or sentence will go beyond the three reasons you may have identified in the past.

CHOOSE TEXTS

Any fiction or nonfiction text could be useful for teaching about an author's reason for including a paragraph or sentence with particular information. But since you may not have asked this question frequently in the past, it may take a while to spot paragraphs and sentences well matched to this question. Get started by looking for paragraphs with a single clear intent. Also look for articles with topic or summary sentences or paragraphs.

The following tools provide practice with concepts important for answering Question 6.3.

PROVIDE PRACTICE USING TOOLS IN CHAPTER 5

- Anchor Chart 30: Analyzing an Author's Purpose for Including a Particular Paragraph or Sentence
- Anchor Chart 3: Explaining Importance in Fiction and Nonfiction

How did this video add to your understanding of _____?

EXPLAIN THE CONCEPT: ANALYZING A VIDEO

Video is a powerful form of text because it contains both words and images, and those words and images come to life right before your eyes. Just like all texts, they are designed for a purpose, and it is your job as a viewer to understand not only *what* the video is explaining, but *how* it is explaining it.

When this question asks how a video adds to your understanding of something, the "something" might be a topic you've studied. Or it could be a story, poem, or article you've read—and now you're watching a video showing the same content. We don't usually think of video (or movies or television) as text because we *watch* them instead of *read* them, but we can get meaning from them in the same way we get meaning from print sources. If we look closely, we may be able to get even more meaning because more of our senses are involved: both seeing and hearing.

The key to the best comprehension is to remember that you're not just looking for "what happens" in the story (which is what you typically focus on when you watch a show). The videos you view as text will be short, just a couple of minutes long. Pay close attention to the message and how the images and other features of the video contribute to that message. If you've also read about the topic or read the same story or poem, compare the two sources. How were they the same or different? Which did you like better? Why?

CHOOSE TEXTS

Remember you are looking for a *short* video, just a couple of minutes long, not a full-length movie. Unlike most movies or television shows students watch, the point here is not just to understand the content. The goal is to recognize how the medium contributes to the message. There are hundreds of websites that meet this need for any discipline or content area. Be sure to choose one approved by your school or district.

The following tool provides practice for answering Question 7.1.

PROVIDE PRACTICE USING TOOLS IN CHAPTER 5

- Anchor Chart 32: Analyzing a Video

Why do you think the author included this illustration (or photograph)?

EXPLAIN THE CONCEPT: ANALYZING AN ILLUSTRATION OR PHOTOGRAPH

Photographs and illustrations included in books and other sources are intended to be more than pretty pictures decorating a page. Sometimes they add details to the information provided in the text. Sometimes the images make you happy or sad or lead to other feelings that you don't get from the words alone. You need to look closely and pay attention to more than just what is happening in the picture. Think about your reaction to the picture and how you feel about it. Think about the mood and how the illustrator or photographer created that mood with details like colors and the expression on people's faces.

CHOOSE TEXTS

Great photographs and illustrations are everywhere! The first place I look for illustrations is picture books, as there are some amazing picture book illustrators (too numerous to list), with art so beautiful I would gladly hang it on my living room wall. Photographs from newspapers past and present are also useful, and easily accessed with a single click. The goal with any image is that it complements the print text in a way that adds meaning. The following tool provides practice for answering Question 7.2.

PROVIDE PRACTICE USING TOOLS IN CHAPTER 5

· Anchor Chart 33: Analyzing a Photograph or Illustration

Which details from [the text] are relevant to the argument that _____?

EXPLAIN THE CONCEPT: FINDING RELEVANT DETAILS

When you're looking for evidence to answer a question, especially when you're reading about an informational topic, sometimes it's tempting to choose the first fact you find. You weren't sure you'd find *any* evidence for your answer, and you're so glad you found something that you write it down quickly and move on. This is not the best approach. The point of this question is to be really picky about your evidence. Evidence must be *relevant*, which means it must be perfectly connected to your topic. Keep reading to the very end of the article or chapter in case the best, most relevant evidence is hiding in the last paragraph. Remember that even when you've found evidence that's relevant, some kinds of evidence are more convincing than others.

CHOOSE TEXTS

Common Core College and Career Readiness Anchor Standard 8 relates only to informational text, so that's the first thing to keep in mind when choosing sources for this question. Beyond that, look for articles that address more than one subtopic within a broader category. For instance, the article as a whole might be about roller coasters. But within the article it might discuss famous roller coasters and roller coaster safety. The question would focus on a single area (perhaps roller coaster safety)—which would determine the relevance of the evidence students cited. I have also noticed that short pieces work as well for this question as longer ones.

Something else to keep in mind for teaching about relevance is that standards-based questions may instead ask, "What details from [the text] are *irrelevant* to the argument that _____?" This is more likely to appear as a selected response rather than a constructed response question. But in your instruction, it would be good to ask students which sentence in a paragraph or portion of a text does *not* support the argument.

The following tools provide practice for answering Question 8.1.

PROVIDE PRACTICE USING TOOLS IN CHAPTER 5

- Anchor Chart 2: Finding Surprising or Helpful Details in an Informational Text
- Anchor Chart 3: Explaining Importance in Fiction and Nonfiction

What additional evidence for _____ could the author have included to make the argument more convincing?

EXPLAIN THE CONCEPT: ADDING RELEVANT DETAILS

To understand what additional evidence could have been added to an explanation, you first need to know the kinds of evidence authors can include when they're writing about a topic to make it both *thorough* and *clear*. Four common kinds of evidence are often included:

- <u>Details</u> like facts and statistics
- <u>Examples</u> to make the idea clearer
- <u>Definitions</u> or explanations of new words
- <u>Quotes</u> from experts

Also remember that evidence is more convincing when it is presented in a way that is easy to understand. Once you've figured out the kind of evidence the author has included (and what was left out), you can suggest ways the author could have made the explanation stronger.

CHOOSE TEXTS

For this question, it might be good to choose a text that students have read and discussed previously—even better if they have identified relevant evidence. This will provide a foundation on which to build. For this reason, I use the same text selected for the question about finding relevant evidence (above) for the sample constructed response about useful additional evidence in Chapter 7.

The following tools provide practice for answering Question 8.2.

PROVIDE PRACTICE USING TOOLS IN CHAPTER 5
- Checklist 3: Critiquing an Explanation
- Anchor Chart 3: Explaining Importance in Fiction and Nonfiction

Which source does a better job of explaining _____? Cite specific evidence to support your answer.

EXPLAIN THE CONCEPT: CRITIQUING SOURCES

Sometimes you will read a book or article on a topic, perhaps something about science or history, and it will seem really confusing. You think, *This is too hard. I don't get it.* You probably think that not understanding is your fault. Of course, that could be true if you didn't read carefully. But there's another possibility that you may be overlooking: Maybe the author didn't explain the information well.

What makes something a *good* explanation? The short answer is that a good explanation is a clear and thorough explanation. When you're reading two sources on the same topic, try to decide which explanation is better, and *why*.

CHOOSE TEXTS

Finding the right sources for this question might take some digging. The first step is to find two texts on the same topic that cover approximately the same content. Then find a specific point addressed by both authors and ask students which explanation they think is better. Using the criteria in Checklist 3: Critiquing an Explanation will offer students a place to start as they decide *why* one explanation is more helpful than another.

The following tools provide practice with concepts important for answering Question 9.1.

PROVIDE PRACTICE USING TOOLS IN CHAPTER 5

- Checklist 3: Critiquing an Explanation
- Anchor Chart 3: Explaining Importance in Fiction and Nonfiction

Explain how each of the selections you read about [topic] could be useful to someone writing about this topic.

EXPLAIN THE CONCEPT: INTEGRATING MULTIPLE SOURCES

One of the problems kids have when writing a report is how to integrate, or put together, information from more than one source. How do you decide what is most useful from each source? There are four main kinds of information you'll want to look for in each source: important vocabulary, facts about the big idea, quotes from experts, and little stories or examples that make the topic feel personal. For instance, if one source has lots of facts, but no stories or examples to show how the facts apply in real life, maybe an example from the second source could be added to make the first source stronger. Remember that for this question, you don't have to write a report or essay. You only need to explain how the different kinds of evidence in both sources would be useful. Also remember to explain the importance of your information.

CHOOSE TEXTS

To find the best resources for responding to this question, look for short articles on the same topic, but with a slightly different focus and with different kinds of evidence. The point is for students to see that different texts give them different kinds of information that they can use when writing reports and essays. Sources don't need to contain all four kinds of information. But try to find selections with more than just facts. Also remember that this question does not ask students to actually write a report or essay based on the information—although you might want to extend the task to include this.

The following tools provide practice with concepts important for answering Question 9.2.

PROVIDE PRACTICE USING TOOLS IN CHAPTER 5

- Anchor Chart 34: Integrating Information from Multiple Sources
- Anchor Chart 3: Explaining Importance in Fiction and Nonfiction

Use the information from these [two] sources to write a diary entry from your point of view, imagining that you are personally experiencing the situation identified in these sources. Be sure to include details from the informational sources you read.

EXPLAIN THE CONCEPT: WRITING FICTION FROM NONFICTION SOURCES

All of the other constructed response questions we've worked on focus on analytical writing. This question calls for narrative writing (a story). It is included here because your answer will be based on *reading*. Often when you write a story, you write about topics you already know a lot about, like an adventure with a friend or a fantasy that comes from your imagination. For these stories, you don't need to read anything before writing. That will not be the case with this question. First you will read information about a topic. Then you will use details you learned to write a fictional piece about that topic. (In this case, the writing will be in the form of a diary entry.) Researching a topic before writing about it is a good skill to learn. Most authors do lots of research before they write a book on any topic.

Since this response asks for a diary entry, it will also be helpful to understand what a diary is and what should be included in a diary entry. A diary is personal writing, almost like talking to a friend. It's a report of what happened in a day or perhaps a longer period of time. Because it is not really intended for anyone else to see, you can be very honest. You can write your thoughts, feelings, and opinions about what you experienced, not just the facts. Since a diary is like a friend, you might begin an entry "Dear Diary." First write a few sentences explaining the events of your day. Then move on to your thoughts, feelings, and opinions. Try to use specific details to make your writing believable. Last piece of advice: Be sure to use details from each source to write your entry. The modeled response will show you how.

CHOOSE TEXTS

Although this is technically a text connection question where students read multiple sources, there's no reason the same question cannot be asked about a single source, especially for younger students. Also, the sample constructed response for this question in Chapter 7 will be especially helpful for this question to illustrate how information can be used for narrative purposes. Be sure to select informational texts with plenty of details students can find easily to work into a piece of narrative writing.

The following tools provide practice with concepts important for answering Question 9.3.

PROVIDE PRACTICE USING TOOLS IN CHAPTER 5

- Checklist 4: Writing a Diary Entry

Identify the central idea in Source #1 and Source #2. Then compare and contrast the way the author develops the central idea in each of the sources.

EXPLAIN THE CONCEPT: COMPARING TEXTS BASED ON CENTRAL IDEA OR OTHER TEXT ELEMENTS

Remember that although this question says "central idea," other terms could be used instead—like *theme, main idea, author's message,* or *lesson.* The answer will be the same regardless of the label that is used. Also, the same answer frame with just a few small modifications can be used for comparing other textual elements such as characters, problem, author's purpose, and more.

Finally, remember that a key word in this question is *develop:* "Compare and contrast the way the author *develops* the central idea in each of the sources." This means you can't just mention a random detail or two to support your claim. Showing the *development* of something requires that you summarize supporting evidence from the beginning, middle, and end of a text to demonstrate how the central idea grew and changed over time. This makes a response to this question longer, more like an essay with multiple paragraphs than a short answer of three or four sentences.

You will probably need four paragraphs for this answer, more if you have additional sources:

Paragraph 1: States the central idea and something important about a similarity or difference between the texts

Paragraph 2: Explains how the author develops the central idea in Source #1

Paragraph 3: Explains how the author develops the central idea in Source #2

Paragraph 4: Explains the importance of the central idea

CHOOSE TEXTS

Any two texts with a similar connection point (central idea, character trait, problem, author's purpose) can be used for this question. Although I used two fables for my modeled response, I also like the idea of mixing genres—for example, a story paired with a poem. You could also use two informational sources. You can see from this response frame that this answer is longer than a typical constructed response, more of an essay. Because they need to show *development*, longer texts will yield longer responses. Keep this in mind when choosing reading selections.

The following tools provide practice with concepts important for answering Question 9.4.

PROVIDE PRACTICE USING TOOLS IN CHAPTER 5

- Anchor Chart 4: Topics and Central Ideas for Narrative Fiction and Nonfiction
- Anchor Chart 35: Comparing Similarities and Differences Between Literary Texts
- Anchor Chart 36: Comparing Similarities and Differences Between Informational Texts
- Anchor Chart 3: Explaining Importance in Fiction and Nonfiction

CHAPTER 5

TOOLS FOR ANALYTICAL READING

LIST OF ANCHOR CHARTS AND CHECKLISTS

- Anchor Chart 1: Finding Surprising or Helpful Details in a Story or Poem
- Anchor Chart 2: Finding Surprising or Helpful Details in an Informational Text
- Anchor Chart 3: Explaining Importance in Fiction and Nonfiction
- Checklist 1: Paraphrasing
- Anchor Chart 4: Topics and Central Ideas for Narrative Fiction and Nonfiction
- Anchor Chart 5: Positive Character Traits and Shades of Meaning
- Anchor Chart 6: Negative Character Traits and Shades of Meaning
- Anchor Chart 7: Positive Character Feelings and Shades of Meaning
- Anchor Chart 8: Negative Character Feelings and Shades of Meaning
- Anchor Chart 9: Positive Character Attitudes and Author's Tone
- Anchor Chart 10: Negative Character Attitudes and Author's Tone
- Anchor Chart 11: Analyzing Character Motivations
- Anchor Chart 12: Analyzing Character Relationships
- Anchor Chart 13: Reasons for a Character's Behavior
- Anchor Chart 14: Comparing Characters
- Anchor Chart 15: How Setting Matters in a Story or Real-Life Event
- Anchor Chart 16: Analyzing the Problem
- Anchor Chart 17: Analyzing Story Parts
- Anchor Chart 18: Analyzing Author's Craft in Narrative Text
- Anchor Chart 19: Analyzing Figurative Language
- Anchor Chart 20: Analyzing a Fable
- Anchor Chart 21: Analyzing a Poem
- Anchor Chart 22: Analyzing Informational Text Features
- Anchor Chart 23: Analyzing Informational Text Structures

How to Model and Practice with Anchor Charts and Checklists

You've explained the concept, but students are still a long way from applying it competently. So, what's next? Modeling and Practicing! With all these anchor charts and checklists!

Let's say the concept is text features and how they add to understanding. (Notice that for all concepts, the goal is never just *identification*, but determining how the concept leads to deeper understanding.) With a text that is a good match for your concept, prepare to show students how they can dig deeper into the concept; in this case, text features. Duplicate the related anchor chart (Anchor Chart 22: Analyzing Informational Text Features) so each student can have their own copy.

Choose a few text features to examine and show students how this would work, modeling with your selected text: "Notice that on this page there's a *text box*. Our chart says that a text box can add meaning or interest. What meaning does *this* text box add?" For this article (let's say it's about sea turtles), students might respond that the text box provides additional details about protecting turtle eggs. Students can fill in the adjacent box: *What it shows in this text*. Be sure to address the issue in the final column too: *How it adds to understanding*. Here, students could mention that the information in the text box about protecting turtle eggs lets them know what they can do to make a difference in saving baby turtles.

Modeling with one example should be enough before sending students off to try applying the concept alone or with a partner. You'll need to make the decision about paired or individual practice based on the students you are teaching. You'll also need to decide how many similar lessons your students need to reinforce the concept before moving on to a written response.

Note that the anchor charts can be photocopied from the book or downloaded and printed from https://wwnorton.com/AwesomeAnswers, for distribution to students.

ANCHOR CHART 1:
FINDING SURPRISING OR HELPFUL DETAILS IN A STORY OR POEM

Source: _____

I am looking for details to show:_____

If you are reading to locate *surprising* details, use Column <u>2</u>. If you are reading to locate *helpful* details, use Column <u>3</u>.

LOOK FOR	EXAMPLE FROM THE TEXT	WHY IT SURPRISED ME	HOW IT HELPED ME UNDERSTAND
Description of the character, problem, or setting Look for odd details that you don't expect. The author included these for a reason!			
Inside thoughts or feelings Look for thoughts that the character is thinking inside their head and sharing with the reader but not other characters. This is a good way to learn what is important to the character.			
Dialogue or word choice What a character *says* also shows what they care about and may give you hints about where they live and even their education.			
Character's actions and small gestures Gestures like rolling your eyes or smiling do a lot to show attitude. Be sure to notice body language and other small actions.			

ANCHOR CHART 2: FINDING SURPRISING OR HELPFUL DETAILS IN AN INFORMATIONAL TEXT

Source: _____

I am looking for details to show: _____

If you are reading to locate *surprising* details, use Column <u>2</u>. If you are reading to locate *helpful* details, use Column <u>3</u>.

EVIDENCE	EXAMPLE FROM THE TEXT	WHY THIS EVIDENCE SURPRISED ME	HOW THIS EVIDENCE HELPED ME UNDERSTAND
Numbers like dates, times, and statistics			
Facts—with proof from reliable sources			
Primary source documents like video, letters, maps, etc.			
Expert opinion—from people you trust			
Examples that *show* rather than *tell* what something is like			
Logical reasoning: Does it make sense?			
Comparisons to something I already understand			
Firsthand experience			
Experimental results			

ANCHOR CHART 3: EXPLAINING IMPORTANCE IN FICTION AND NONFICTION

Source: _____

Choose <u>one</u> of the reasons in the left column that would work well to explain the importance of evidence in your text. Fill in the right column with an example that connects this reason to your text.

WHY EVIDENCE MIGHT BE IMPORTANT	QUESTIONS TO ASK YOURSELF ABOUT EACH AREA OF IMPORTANCE	HOW I WOULD EXPLAIN IMPORTANCE FOR *THIS* TEXT (CHOOSE 1)
You have a personal connection	Have you had experience with the same character trait (lesson, problem, or whatever) in your own life? How was your response the same or different from that of the character? How might it be different in the future?	
There are possible consequences	For whom will this character trait, lesson, problem, or information matter? What might happen because of the character's or person's actions?	
Other people may have a strong reaction to this story or information	What might other people say about this character's or person's response to this situation? Why? How does that compare to *your* response?	
It teaches an important life lesson	Has the character's or person's actions helped you figure out anything about what's important in life? What is it?	
Action is needed!	Can you take a step yourself to make a difference with this issue? Can someone else?	

CHECKLIST 1: PARAPHRASING

Source: _____

Use this checklist to guide you as you paraphrase a short passage. Check each statement if you have done what it advised.

☐ I read the passage several times to make sure I **understand** it.

☐ I underlined or jotted down words I need to **keep**. These might be names of things like people, places, dates, and titles.

☐ I underlined or jotted down words I want to **change**. These will be words that have synonyms. I might want to check a thesaurus to choose synonyms.

☐ I noted sentences or phrases I might want to **rearrange** or **combine**.

☐ I wrote my own version of the passage **without looking at the original**. I was careful to start my first sentence differently from the first sentence in the original passage.

☐ I **checked** my version against the original to make sure I got all of the meaning and didn't leave anything out.

ANCHOR CHART 4: TOPICS AND CENTRAL IDEAS FOR NARRATIVE FICTION AND NONFICTION

Source: _____

Identify the topic first. Then determine the central idea (from Column 2). Or think of a different central idea matched to your topic.

TOPICS	POSSIBLE CENTRAL IDEAS	MORE CENTRAL IDEAS
Courage	• We need courage to face problems • Showing courage is a characteristic of a leader	
Friendship	• Know who your *real* friends are • Friends support each other • Building friendships is hard work • A friend can help you feel less lonely	
Identity	• Be yourself • Be happy with what you have • Follow your heart instead of following the crowd	
Family	• Family is important • Families are made in many ways • It's important to build relationships with family members—including grandparents and extended family	
Growing Up	• Growing up offers many challenges—such as school, family life, siblings, and issues with friends • Kids need support and guidance from people like parents and teachers as they face problems growing up	

TOPICS	POSSIBLE CENTRAL IDEAS	MORE CENTRAL IDEAS
Self-control	• Self-control is important to solving problems • Anger can lead to losing self-control	
Suffering	• Many problems can lead to suffering—like poverty, addiction, sickness, death of someone special, prejudice, physical and other differences • Do your part to end the suffering of others	
Persistence	• You need to work hard to succeed • The bigger the challenge, the harder you need to work • Leaders often demonstrate persistence	
Kindness	• Treat everyone (including animals) with kindness and respect • We all have kindness to give • If you are kind to someone, they may be kind to you in return	
Honesty	• Be honest, even when it's difficult • *How* you tell the truth makes a big difference to people's feelings	
Hope	• Never lose hope that better times will come • Hope helps you survive bad situations	

TOPICS	POSSIBLE CENTRAL IDEAS	MORE CENTRAL IDEAS
Love	• Everyone needs to be loved • We all show love in different ways • Don't be afraid to show your love for someone	
Creativity and Resourcefulness	• Using your imagination and your initiative can help to solve problems • Using your imagination and your initiative can make life more fun and interesting	
Leadership	• Anyone can be a leader • Many qualities are important to good leadership: honesty, active listening, creative thinking, confidence, communication, vision, trust, compassion, taking a stand, courage, and more	
Freedom	• We pay a price for freedom • People who are free can make their own choices • Freedom makes your heart happy	
Other		
Other		
Other		

ANCHOR CHART 5: POSITIVE CHARACTER TRAITS AND SHADES OF MEANING

Source: _____

First identify the <u>character trait</u>. Then look for a more precise <u>shade of meaning</u> in the next column. In the last column, identify an example from the text.

POSITIVE CHARACTER TRAIT	SHADES OF MEANING	TEXT EXAMPLE
Kind	Generous, loving, compassionate, loyal, thoughtful, considerate, friendly, helpful, agreeable, respectful, forgiving, joyful, patient, empathetic	
Determined	Persevering, persistent, hardworking, energetic, studious, grit, resourceful, independent, clever, wise, creative	
Honest	Integrity, humble, serious, trustworthy, fair, responsible, sensitive, truthful	
Brave	Courageous, self-confident, fun-loving, daring, adventurous, bold	

ANCHOR CHART 6: NEGATIVE CHARACTER TRAITS AND SHADES OF MEANING

Source: _____

First identify the <u>character trait</u>. Then look for a more precise <u>shade of meaning</u> in the next column. In the last column, identify an example from the text.

NEGATIVE CHARACTER TRAIT	SHADES OF MEANING	TEXT EXAMPLE
Mean	Bossy, conceited, cruel, disagreeable, greedy, nagging, quarrelsome, rude, selfish, stingy, vengeful, nosy	
Lazy	Careless, reckless, apathetic, uninvolved, dull, disinterested	
Dishonest	Sneaky, shrewd, spiteful	
Fearful	Cowardly, timid, overly cautious	

ANCHOR CHART 7: POSITIVE CHARACTER FEELINGS AND SHADES OF MEANING

Source: _____

First identify the character feeling. Then look for a more precise shade of meaning in the next column. In the last column, identify an example from the text.

POSITIVE FEELING	SHADES OF MEANING	TEXT EXAMPLE
Happy	Content, glad, cheery, ecstatic, delighted, excited, peaceful, proud, worthy, satisfied, elated, lucky, proud	
Accepted	Liked, respected, powerful, recognized	
Hopeful	Optimistic, positive, invincible, trusting	
Curious	Inquisitive, interested	

ANCHOR CHART 8: NEGATIVE CHARACTER FEELINGS AND SHADES OF MEANING

Source: _____

First identify the <u>character feeling</u>. Then look for a more precise <u>shade of meaning</u> in the next column. In the last column, identify an example from the text.

NEGATIVE FEELING	SHADES OF MEANING	TEXT EXAMPLE
Sad	Gloomy, forlorn, depressed, disappointed, sorrowful, miserable, bored, devastated, embarrassed, grief-stricken, indifferent, stunned	
Worried	Anxious, nervous, troubled, concerned, frightened, guilty, confused, perplexed, skeptical, suspicious, terrified, vulnerable	
Rejected	Alienated, excluded, disrespected, hurt (feelings), humiliated, ignored, inferior, jealous, lonely, powerless, ashamed, neglected	
Angry	Annoyed, irritated, livid, outraged, furious, frustrated, resentful, bitter	

ANCHOR CHART 9: POSITIVE CHARACTER ATTITUDES AND AUTHOR'S TONE

Source: _____

For a character with a positive attitude or a positive author tone, first identify the attitude or tone. Then identify an example from the text that shows this attitude or tone.

This character (or person): _____ had a mostly POSITIVE attitude.

I WOULD DESCRIBE THIS POSITIVE ATTITUDE AS	AN EXAMPLE FROM THE TEXT
Determined: Believes in hard work and is willing to keep trying	
Optimistic (or hopeful): Looks on the bright side, even when times are tough	
Humble: Tries hard, but doesn't brag about their own success or achievements	
Considerate: Thinks about other people's needs when making choices	
Appreciative: Expresses sincere thanks to people who lend a helping hand	
Responsible: Tries to be dependable and follows through on doing what is right	
Welcoming: Shows respect for everyone, regardless of differences	
Admiring: Thinks highly of someone based on their accomplishments or a personal strength	
Other	

ANCHOR CHART 10: NEGATIVE CHARACTER ATTITUDES AND AUTHOR'S TONE

Source: _____

For a character with a negative attitude or a negative author tone, first identify the attitude or tone. Then identify an example from the text that shows this attitude or tone.

This character (or person): _____ had a mostly NEGATIVE attitude.

I WOULD DESCRIBE THIS NEGATIVE ATTITUDE AS	AN EXAMPLE FROM THE TEXT
Defeated: Gives up easily without really trying to succeed	
Pessimistic: Expects the worst from life, like nothing will ever work out in a good way	
Superior: Thinks they are better than other people and may put other people down	
Self-centered: Always thinks of themselves first without caring about others' needs	
Irresponsible: Sometimes reckless or unreliable; doesn't make good choices	
Prejudiced: Discriminates based on race, gender, or something else that divides people	
Angry: Feels very displeased; furious; annoyed	
Other	

ANCHOR CHART 11: ANALYZING CHARACTER MOTIVATIONS

Source: _____

First decide whether the character is motivated by a basic need, something they want, or a feeling or value. Then choose a more specific need, want, or value. Identify an example from the text that shows this motivation.

THINGS THAT MOTIVATE PEOPLE TO ACT AND BEHAVE AS THEY DO	SPECIFIC THINGS THAT MOTIVATE PEOPLE WITHIN DIFFERENT CATEGORIES	WHAT MOTIVATES *THIS* PERSON?
Basic needs	Such as survival, safety, warmth, or food	
Wants	Such as respect, recognition, fitting in, achievement, fear of failing, friendship, money (or something money can buy), revenge, a personal goal, creating something, knowing the truth, power, praise	
Feelings and values	Such as love, caring, compassion, loyalty, jealousy, fear, integrity, curiosity, honor, justice	

ANCHOR CHART 12: ANALYZING CHARACTER RELATIONSHIPS

Source: _____

Analyzing the relationship between _____ and _____
                                    CHARACTER 1   CHARACTER 2

First decide if the relationship is <u>positive</u> or <u>negative</u>. Then choose <u>one</u> relationship word and give an example.

POSITIVE RELATIONSHIPS: CHARACTERS THINK, SPEAK, AND ACT IN WAYS THAT ARE:	TEXT EXAMPLE
Loving	
Nurturing	
Respectful	
Kind	
Caring	

NEGATIVE RELATIONSHIPS: ONE OR MORE CHARACTERS BEHAVE IN WAYS THAT ARE:	TEXT EXAMPLE
Dishonest (instead of honest, trustworthy)	
Abusive, mean, bullying (instead of kind)	
Neglectful (instead of caring or nurturing)	
Cruel (instead of kind or loving)	
Jealous (instead of supportive)	
Taking advantage (instead of loyal)	

ANCHOR CHART 13: REASONS FOR A CHARACTER'S BEHAVIOR

Source: _____

Character: _____

There is more than one reason for a character's behavior. Choose <u>three</u> reasons you think are most important in determining *this* character's behavior. Then choose an example from the text for each reason that shows this.

REASONS FOR A CHARACTER'S BEHAVIOR	REASONS FOR *THIS* CHARACTER'S BEHAVIOR
Does the character have a clear **goal** and a **plan** to achieve the goal? If so, what is the goal? What is the plan?	
Has the character caused the **problem** or made it worse in any way, or has someone caused the problem for them?	
What are the character's **skills**? What does the character do well—or not so well?	
What does the character **need or want**? Is it a basic *need* like food and a place to live? Or is it something she *wants* like friendship or loyalty?	
What does the character **care** about: Himself/herself, family members and close friends, other people around the world?	
Is the character's **attitude** mostly positive or mostly negative? What words, thoughts, or actions show this?	

REASONS FOR A CHARACTER'S BEHAVIOR	REASONS FOR *THIS* CHARACTER'S BEHAVIOR
What are the character's **feelings:** Happy, worried, surprised, confident, love, something else?	
What's the **backstory:** Does the character come from a past where he or she has been supported, respected, and nurtured? Or, has the character faced discrimination, disrespect, and hardships?	
Does the character **change** throughout the story? How?	

ANCHOR CHART 14: COMPARING CHARACTERS

Source: _____

For comparing two characters, choose at least two reasons (like goal, skills, or needs) that are important in the story, and show how they are the same or different for these characters.

REASONS FOR A CHARACTER'S BEHAVIOR	CHARACTER A: _____	CHARACTER B: _____
Goal and plan		
Cause of the problem		
Character's skills		
What the character needs or wants		
What the character cares about		
Character's attitude		
Character's feelings		
Character's background		
Does the character change?		

**ANCHOR CHART 15: HOW SETTING MATTERS
IN A STORY OR REAL-LIFE EVENT**

Source: _____

Fill in all boxes to analyze the setting in your text. Think carefully about the last box describing how the situation would change in a different time or place.

POINTS TO CONSIDER	TEXT EXAMPLE
What is the situation? Is it real or fictional?	
When does the story or event take place?	
Where does the story or event take place?	
How does this specific time and place matter to this situation: How would it have been different in another time or place? (Think about laws and what people believed at the time and in this place.)	

ANCHOR CHART 16: ANALYZING THE PROBLEM

Source: _____

Circle one choice in each section. In the next column, give an example from the text that supports your answer.

WHAT KIND OF PROBLEM IS IT? WHAT IS THE PROBLEM?	
Problem with self	
Problem with another person	
Problem with nature	

WHEN DID THE PROBLEM GET STARTED? HOW DOES THE AUTHOR INTRODUCE IT?	
At the beginning of the story	
Before this story started	
After the author describes the way life used to be before this problem began	

WHAT HAPPENS WITH THE PROBLEM AFTER THE AUTHOR INTRODUCES IT?	
It starts to get solved right away with these steps:	
It gets worse before it gets better because these things happen:	

HOW DOES THE PROBLEM GET SOLVED IN THE END?	
The characters solve the problem themselves. Here's what happens:	
The characters solve the problem with help. Here's what happens:	
There is progress toward solving the problem, but the problem still exists. Here's what happens:	

ANCHOR CHART 17: ANALYZING STORY PARTS

Source: _____

Fill in each box with information about the story you read.

STORY PARTS	ANALYZING PARTS OF *THIS* STORY		
Characters	Who are the important characters? Does anyone change during the story? How?		
Setting	Where and when does the story take place?		
Problem	What problem or conflict gets the story started?		
Actions	What happens to try to solve the problem? (There might be more than three actions)		
	1.	2.	3.
Outcome	What happens at the end to resolve the problem? (The problem might get <u>solved</u>, or there might just be <u>progress</u> toward the goal.)		
Ending	How does the story end? (What happens beyond solving the problem?)		

ANCHOR CHART 18: ANALYZING AUTHOR'S CRAFT IN NARRATIVE TEXT

Source: _____

For each author's craft you find in your source, identify an example from the text and explain why you think the author included it.

AUTHOR'S CRAFT	WHAT IT IS	EXAMPLE FROM *THIS* TEXT	HOW IT ADDS TO UNDERSTANDING	WHY THE AUTHOR CHOSE TO INCLUDE IT
Description	Single words, full sentences, or paragraphs that provide details about a character, the setting, or an event in the story; may include strong verbs and precise nouns, figurative language, adjectives and adverbs		Helps the reader picture what the author is saying and sets the tone of the writing	
Dialogue	Conversation between two or more characters		Shows what is important to individual characters or shows the relationship between characters; can show attitude of characters	

Inside thoughts	The thoughts a character is thinking inside their head that the reader sees, but are not shared with the other characters; often seen in stories with a first person narrator		Shows how a character is interpreting what is happening or what is important to the character	
Gesture	Small actions or body language like rolling your eyes, sighing, smiling, jumping for joy, and others		Shows the attitude of the character about something that is currently happening in the story	
Other				

ANCHOR CHART 19: ANALYZING FIGURATIVE LANGUAGE

Source: _____

Give an example of different kinds of figurative language in your text and explain why you think the author included each one.

LANGUAGE	EXAMPLES	EXAMPLE FROM *THIS* TEXT	WHY THE AUTHOR PROBABLY INCLUDED IT
Idiom: An expression where the word meaning is not exactly what the words *say*	She has a <u>frog in her throat</u>. It is <u>raining cats and dogs</u>.		
Simile: A comparison using *like* or *as*	I ran <u>like the wind</u>. I ran <u>as fast as a speeding train</u>.		
Metaphor: A comparison of one thing to another without using *like* or *as*	The lawn is <u>a green carpet.</u> The road was <u>a ribbon of black</u>.		
Personification: Giving a nonliving thing human characteristics to describe it	The <u>wind howled</u> in the night. The <u>flowers were crying</u> for water.		
Hyperbole: An exaggeration that is often extreme and sometimes humorous	I was so tired <u>I wanted to sleep for a month</u>. He jumped <u>a hundred feet</u> into the air.		

ANCHOR CHART 20: ANALYZING A FABLE

Source: _____

Fill in each box with evidence from the fable you read. Although these story elements are in most stories, Column 2 explains how they apply to fables.

STORY ELEMENTS	WHAT YOU USUALLY FIND IN A FABLE	WHAT YOU FIND IN *THIS* FABLE
Characters	Although the characters are usually animals or mythical creatures, they act and talk like humans. There are usually no more than 2 or 3 characters and they have a single good or bad trait. Sometimes the trait is common to the animal. For example, an owl might be wise; a lion might be brave. In some fables, the characters are people or even objects like the sun or wind.	
Setting	A fable can take place anywhere. Lots of fables take place outside because nature often plays an important role.	
Problem	Because fables are short, there is just one main problem or situation.	
Resolution	The good character always wins—due to their positive trait.	
Ending	Most fables contain a moral or lesson at the end, although sometimes this may be left out so readers can identify it themselves.	
Tone	Sometimes fables seem humorous because the "bad character" behaves foolishly, which readers find funny.	
Other special features unique to this genre	A fable is usually quite short, just a paragraph or two. Many fables are very old, supposedly told by Aesop. However, there are modern fables, too. Some stories by Dr. Seuss are fables, such as *The Lorax* and *Yertle the Turtle*.	

ANCHOR CHART 21: ANALYZING A POEM

Source: _____

Complete these sections in order: Sounds Different, Looks Different, Language, Intent.

POETRY *SOUNDS* DIFFERENT FROM OTHER WRITING

Poetry sounds different from other writing. It sounds almost like music when you read it out loud because it has a **rhythm** that comes from the pattern of the words. Not all poems **rhyme**, but many do. Rhyming words at the end of a line also add to a poem's musical quality. Something else that adds to the sound of some poems is **alliteration**, which means that two or more words next to each other begin with the same sound. Poets can make their words sound **soft** or **hard** by the words they choose. For example, *crackle* sounds hard when you say it, while *shimmer* sounds softer.

FEATURES THAT MAKE WRITING SOUND LIKE A POEM	FEATURES THAT MAKE *THIS* WRITING SOUND LIKE A POEM
Rhythm	
Rhyme	
Alliteration	
Soft words	
Hard words	

POETRY *LOOKS* DIFFERENT FROM OTHER WRITING

Poetry is arranged differently from other writing. Instead of paragraphs, there are **stanzas**. Instead of sentences there are **lines**. For punctuation, there are often **commas** at the end of a line, rather than periods. Sometimes poets change the **order** of words so they're different from what you expect. This makes certain words and ideas stand out. A poet also uses **line breaks** to make ideas stand out. When a line ends where you don't expect it to end, it lets you know what words a poet wants you to notice. Some lines may be only one or two words long for this purpose. A poet might **repeat** lines or words, too. This also lets you know the thoughts that are the most important.

FEATURES THAT MAKE WRITING LOOK LIKE A POEM	FEATURES THAT MAKE *THIS* WRITING LOOK LIKE A POEM
Stanzas	
Lines	
Punctuation (lots of commas)	
The order of words is sometimes different from what you expect	
Line breaks show which words to emphasize	

THE *LANGUAGE* OF POETRY IS OFTEN DIFFERENT FROM THE LANGUAGE OF OTHER WRITING

All writing uses these language features sometimes. But poetry uses them often. For example, **imagery** is important to poetry, which means that the poet uses words that help readers make pictures in their mind or imagine the taste, touch, sound, or scent of something. This may include **figures of speech** like personification, metaphors, similes, and hyperbole. Sometimes poems that were written a long time ago are harder to understand because the language is **archaic** (which is a fancy way of saying "old-fashioned").

FEATURES THAT MAKE THE LANGUAGE OF POETRY DIFFERENT FROM THE LANGUAGE OF OTHER WRITING	FEATURES THAT MAKE THE LANGUAGE OF *THIS* WRITING POETIC
Imagery	
Figures of speech	
Archaic language	

THE *INTENT* OF POETRY IS TO APPEAL TO YOUR *FEELINGS* AS WELL AS YOUR THINKING

Poets choose to write a poem about something rather than a story or article because they want to express strong **feelings** about their topic, and they want the poem to prompt you to have strong feelings, too. Many poems have a **serious** tone, and the poet tries to make you feel the love, beauty, sadness, or other emotion. Other poems are **just-for-fun** (like poems by Shel Silverstein) and the poet wants you to laugh or enjoy the silliness. Either way, the author uses **imagination** to express ideas in a very personal way. Poems usually have one **big idea** that they are trying to communicate. Always look for this big idea.

FEATURES THAT MAKE THE INTENT OF POETRY DIFFERENT FROM OTHER WRITING	FEATURES THAT MAKE THE INTENT OF *THIS* POEM DIFFERENT FROM OTHER WRITING
Feelings expressed in this poem	
This poem has a serious tone	
This is a "just-for-fun" poem	
This poem shows imagination	
This poem has a big idea	

ANCHOR CHART 22: ANALYZING INFORMATIONAL TEXT FEATURES

Source: _____

Find text features in the informational source you are reading. Then complete the two columns for what each text feature shows and how it adds to your understanding.

TEXT FEATURE	WHAT IT SHOWS	WHAT IT SHOWS IN *THIS* TEXT	HOW IT ADDS TO UNDERSTANDING
Table of Contents	Gives a list of topics and page numbers so information can be found quickly.		
Photographs and Other Illustrations	Pictures taken with a camera that show what something looks like in real life.		
Captions	Words under a photograph or illustration explaining it.		
Labels	Words that describe parts of a map, chart, or other text feature.		
Headings	The title or name given to a section/chapter of a book so you know what it will be about.		
Charts and Tables	Show information in a different way that is more visual.		
Diagrams	A drawing or model that shows or explains something.		

Textboxes and sidebars	A box or some other shape that contains text that adds meaning or interest.		
Cutaways	A picture of what something looks like on the inside—like you're slicing through it.		
Fonts of different size, color, and style	Print can be bold, different colors, fonts, and sizes—to make certain words stand out.		
Glossary	Located at the back of the book—includes words and definitions.		
Index	Located at the back of the book—includes main topics and page numbers.		
Close-Ups	Photographs that have been zoomed in or enlarged so you can see the details.		
Maps	A picture showing different regions of the Earth. There are many kinds of maps.		
Bullet Points	Small dot followed by information often in short phrases; presented in list form—to help you focus on important points.		

ANCHOR CHART 23: ANALYZING INFORMATIONAL TEXT STRUCTURES

Source: _____

Use the explanation, example, and reason for each text structure to help you answer the two questions at the end of this chart.

TEXT STRUCTURE	WHAT IT IS	EXAMPLES OF WHERE YOU MIGHT FIND IT	REASON WHY YOU MIGHT CHOOSE IT
Description	Gives readers a detailed description of something, probably with different main ideas and details, headings, and subheadings	"All about" books (like "All About Horses" or "Understanding Organic Gardening")	If you wanted to explain a lot about a topic that has different subtopics or categories of information
Cause/Effect	Shows the cause of a situation, and what happens because of it. There could be several causes that lead to one effect (or situation), or a cause could set off a series of effects	Sometimes news articles use this structure—for example, a hurricane leads to deaths, homelessness, power outages, and more	If you wanted to show what the outcome of an action might be
Compare/Contrast	Compares similarities and differences between two or more people, ideas, or something else	Editorials, opinion pieces, and advertisements are some of the text formats that show differences between two choices—often to justify a point of view	If you wanted to analyze the differences between two people, ideas, etc., perhaps convincing someone that one point of view is better than another

Sequence	Shows events that happen in a particular order leading to an outcome, but not focused on a solution to a problem	"How to" books; instructions for how to make something; life cycle books	If you wanted to explain something where the order of events or steps was important
Problem/ Solution	Shows a problem and possible solutions—or shows one or more actual solutions to how a problem was solved	Current events; history books; historical fiction; science books	If you wanted to show what *could* happen or what *did* happen based on an important world problem or action
Narrative Nonfiction	Shows information in story form, perhaps with fictional elements as in historical fiction, or the life of an animal	Biographies, memoirs, stories about the lives of animals, historical fiction	If you wanted to make the information more interesting or memorable, or if you wanted to include more personal details

The structure of *this* text or part of the text is _____

_____.

I think the author chose this structure because _____

_____

_____.

ANCHOR CHART 24: ANALYZING THE KIND OF INFORMATION THE AUTHOR INCLUDES IN A [PARAGRAPH]

Source: _____

Choose <u>one</u> answer for your text (either a literary or informational source). Then complete the responses at the bottom of this page.

LITERARY TEXT	INFORMATIONAL TEXT
Is the author introducing a character?	Is the author offering a reason or evidence for something or defending a claim?
Is the author showing the relationship between characters?	Is the author introducing a new topic or subtopic?
Is the author giving more information about a character such as their motivation, attitude, or what they look like?	Is the author giving more explanation of an earlier point, or giving an example?
Is the author describing the setting?	Is the author showing a cause or an effect?
Is the author introducing the problem or giving you more information about the problem?	Is the author describing the problem or the solution to the problem?
Is the author comparing or contrasting?	Is the author giving an opinion or stating a fact?
Is the author showing the lesson a character learned?	Is the author including expert knowledge (maybe a quote from a primary source)?
Is the author building suspense?	Is the author comparing and contrasting?
Is the author showing the thought in a character's head?	Is the author describing something?
Other?	Other?

The purpose of this [paragraph] is to _____

_____

Evidence from the text that shows this is _____

_____

ANCHOR CHART 25: ANALYZING HOW PARTS OF A TEXT FIT TOGETHER

Source: _____

Check the box in Column 1 that best applies to the designated [paragraph]. Then answer the questions for Column 2 and Column 3 on the lines below.

1 HOW DOES THIS [PARAGRAPH] FIT INTO THE INFORMATION AROUND IT?	2 EVIDENCE FROM THE TEXT	3 WHAT *I* THINK
The [paragraph] <u>introduces</u> the selection	What does it introduce?	Do you think this is a good introduction? Why or why not?
The [paragraph] offers <u>details</u> about information explained in the previous [paragraph]	What details does the next paragraph include?	Did the author choose relevant details?
The [paragraph] gives an <u>example</u> of something explained in the previous [paragraph]	What example does the [paragraph] provide?	Did the author give an example that was easy to understand? Explain.
The [paragraph] introduces a <u>new topic</u>	What is the new topic?	How well does the new topic fit with the information that came before?
The [paragraph] is the <u>next step</u> in a process	What is the next step?	How does this step fit with the steps that came before?
The [paragraph] draws a <u>conclusion</u> from the rest of the selection	What is the conclusion?	Do you think this is a good way to end the selection? Explain.

Evidence from the text: _____

_____

What I think: _____

_____

ANCHOR CHART 26: ANALYZING HOW AN AUTHOR BEGINS A STORY

Source: _____

Choose <u>one</u> or <u>two</u> points from the first column. Then fill in the two columns next to your choices to explain your reasoning.

HOW THE STORY BEGINS	WHY THE AUTHOR PROBABLY CHOSE TO BEGIN THE STORY THIS WAY	WHY I LIKE OR DON'T LIKE THIS BEGINNING
It gives background information that readers will find interesting.		
It describes the setting so readers can picture it in their mind.		
It begins with dialogue which gets readers interested in the characters.		
It begins with action that shows the story will be exciting.		
It asks questions that will be answered in the rest of the story.		
The author shares a detail that is mysterious and makes you want to find the answer.		
The narrator introduces themself to the reader in a surprising way.		

ANCHOR CHART 27: ANALYZING HOW AN AUTHOR ENDS A STORY

Source: _____

Choose <u>one</u> or <u>two</u> points from the first column. Then fill in the two columns next to your choices to explain your reasoning.

HOW THE STORY ENDS	WHY THE AUTHOR PROBABLY CHOSE THIS ENDING	WHY I LIKE OR DON'T LIKE THIS ENDING
There is a "twist." The ending is surprising because you didn't expect this outcome.		
It's an unhappy ending. What you've been fearing all along actually happens.		
The antagonist finally sees that they've been badly behaved and becomes well-behaved.		
It's a happy ending, but might be a little bit sad, too.		
The ending is *ambiguous*, which means it can be interpreted in different ways.		
The story ends quickly after the problem has been solved because the adventure is over.		
The author or character adds a "life lesson" or moral—in case you missed the central idea.		

ANCHOR CHART 28: ANALYZING A FLASHBACK

Source: _____

Fill in each box below about the flashback in your text.

Where is the flashback in the text: **Beginning   Middle   End**

In one or two sentences explain the flashback in your own words

THE PURPOSE OF THE FLASHBACK (CHOOSE 1)	HOW DOES THE FLASHBACK SHOW THIS?
The character or person feels afraid, nervous, worried, excited, happy, or some other feeling—based on something that happened in the past that led to the same feeling now.	
The character or person faced a problem in the past that had to be overcome—and made them a stronger person as a result.	
The character or person dreamed about something that eventually came true—or didn't come true.	
The character or person did something that they now regret.	
Other:	

ANCHOR CHART 29: ANALYZING A BACKSTORY

Source: _____

Fill in each box below about the backstory in your text.

Where is the backstory in the text: **Beginning**   **Middle**   **End**

In one or two sentences explain the backstory in your own words

THE PURPOSE OF THE BACKSTORY (CHOOSE 1)	HOW DOES THE BACKSTORY SHOW THIS?
The author wants to show that life was better before this problem arose.	
The author wants to show that life was more challenging in the past than it is now.	
The author wants to show how someone has changed.	
The author wants to show why someone reacts to a problem the way they do.	
Other:	

ANCHOR CHART 30: ANALYZING A QUOTE FROM ANOTHER AUTHOR AT THE BEGINNING OF A BOOK OR CHAPTER

Source: _____

Fill in each box below about the quote from another author in your text.

Where is the quote by another author in the text: **Beginning   Middle   End**

In one or two sentences explain the quote by another author in your own words

THE PURPOSE OF QUOTE FROM ANOTHER AUTHOR AT THE BEGINNING OF A BOOK OR CHAPTER (CHOOSE 1)	HOW DOES THE QUOTE FROM A DIFFERENT AUTHOR SHOW THIS?
The author wants to make a connection to the central idea of the book or chapter.	
The author wants to let us know we'll be finding out more about a character, problem, setting, or something else important to the story.	
The author wants to give us hints about what will happen in the book or chapter.	
Other:	

ANCHOR CHART 31: ANALYZING AN AUTHOR'S PURPOSE FOR INCLUDING A PARTICULAR PARAGRAPH OR SENTENCE

Source: _____

Choose <u>one</u> purpose from the first column and then fill in the box next to it.

AUTHOR'S PURPOSE FOR INCLUDING A PARAGRAPH OR SENTENCE	WHY THE AUTHOR INCLUDED THIS PARAGRAPH OR SENTENCE
Describe something or someone	
Give examples of something	
Explain or define something	
Introduce a topic	
Summarize a topic	
Support something with evidence	
Show similarities or differences	
Transition to a new topic	
Agree or disagree with something	
Restate something with different words	
Give an opinion about something	

CHECKLIST 2: DEFENDING A POINT OF VIEW

Source: _____

Check items in this list to show the guidelines you followed in defending your point of view. Then complete the statements at the bottom of this page.

☐ I introduced my argument by identifying the issue (problem) and clearly stating my position (point of view) about it.

☐ I chose my strongest reason and explained it first.

☐ I used evidence from the text to support my reason.

☐ I gave another reason for my position.

☐ I used evidence from the text to support my second reason.

☐ If there were other reasons for my position, I included them and supporting evidence.

☐ I shared the opposing point of view and explained why I think it is wrong.

☐ I explained why it is important to find a solution to this problem.

I think the <u>strongest</u> part of my answer is _____

_____ because _____

_____

I think I still need to work on _____

_____ because _____

_____.

ANCHOR CHART 32: ANALYZING A VIDEO

Title of video: _____

For any video you watch, try to fill in as many of these boxes as possible.

THE TOPIC	
Summarize what the video shows and what you learned about this topic.	
What are the key words?	

THE MESSAGE	
What is the message?	
What is the purpose of the message?	
What is the point of view of the people who created the video?	

THE MEDIUM	
What do you consider the most powerful images? Why?	
Who is most represented in this video? Who is least represented (gender, culture, race, age, other)?	
What other features of this video (like music, the narration or color) added to meaning? How?	
If you've read about this same topic in a book or other source, how does the video compare? What do you like better or not as well? Why?	

ANCHOR CHART 33: ANALYZING A PHOTOGRAPH OR ILLUSTRATION

Photograph or illustration: _____

When analyzing a photograph or illustration, complete as many of these boxes as possible.

ANSWER ALL FOUR THESE QUESTIONS IN YOUR ANSWER	
What do you see in this photograph or illustration?	
What feeling do you get from this photograph or illustration? Explain.	
What do you understand based on this photograph or illustration that you did *not* realize from just reading the text that goes with it?	
Why do you think the author or illustrator included this photograph or illustration?	
ANSWER AT LEAST ONE OF THE QUESTIONS BELOW IN YOUR ANSWER	
What is the mood of this photograph or illustration? How does the image create this mood?	
If the photograph or illustration is the cover image of the text, why do you think *this* picture was chosen?	
What colors do you notice in the photograph or illustration? Why do the colors matter?	
Is there anything about this photograph or illustration that you think misrepresents the subject or promotes stereotypes?	
What questions do you have based on this photograph or illustration?	

CHECKLIST 3: CRITIQUING AN EXPLANATION

Source: _____

Mark the sentences below to show what is true for this explanation of:

_____

Kinds of evidence

☐ The author included plenty of <u>details</u> (like facts and statistics) to give me a thorough understanding of the topic.

☐ The author gave one or more <u>examples</u> (or stories) to make the idea clearer.

☐ The author <u>defined or explained</u> hard words to make them clearer.

☐ The author included <u>quotes from experts</u> to support the claim.

How the evidence is presented

☐ It was easy to recognize the central idea because there was a topic sentence.

☐ The author made new ideas clear by comparing them to something familiar to me.

☐ The author used sentences that weren't too long or confusing.

☐ The author showed how ideas fit together.

☐ The author gave me new information, but not so much that I felt overwhelmed.

This explanation was mostly easy/difficult to understand because_____

_____

It could have been clearer and more thorough if the author _____

_____

ANCHOR CHART 34: INTEGRATING INFORMATION FROM MULTIPLE SOURCES

Source: _____

Provide evidence from each source to fill in all boxes in both columns. (This will show you the information that needs to be combined.)

INFORMATION INCLUDED IN EACH TEXT	SOURCE 1	SOURCE 2
Introduction		
Words defined or explained		
Facts that support the big idea		
Quotes or advice from experts		
Stories or examples that add human interest to the topic		
Conclusion: Summing it up and explaining importance		

CHECKLIST 4: WRITING A DIARY ENTRY

Source: _____

Check items in this list to show the guidelines you followed in writing your diary entry.

☐ I began my diary entry with the date (and location if appropriate).

☐ I used a greeting like "Dear Diary" or something else to get started.

☐ I started my entry by explaining the events or what happened.

☐ I wrote in the first person (*I, me, we*—not *he, she, her, him*).

☐ I used the past tense (I *walked*, not I *walk* or I *will walk*).

☐ I included thoughts and feelings.

☐ I included both facts and opinions.

☐ I used language that paints a picture in readers' minds (like strong verbs, specific nouns, and great adjectives).

☐ I used an informal tone that sounds like talking, and my writing sounds honest.

☐ I ended with something like "Love," or "Your friend," and then my name.

ANCHOR CHART 35: COMPARING SIMILARITIES AND DIFFERENCES BETWEEN LITERARY TEXTS

Source 1: _____

Source 2: _____

Fill in each box for both of your sources.

TEXT ELEMENTS	ANALYZING LITERARY ELEMENTS	SOURCE 1	SOURCE 2
Goals	What is the goal of each character? Did the characters in both (all) texts have the same goal or different goals?		
Plot Development	How does the author show you what's happening in the story: Lots of dialogue, description, thoughts in the character's head, other?		
Motivation	What motivated each character? What did each one care about?		
Attitudes	What was each character's attitude? Were their attitudes the same or different?		
Solving the Problem	Did anyone have help solving the problem, or did they solve the problem alone? Was someone else in the story working against them?		
Learning the Lesson	Did both (all) characters learn the lesson the hard way, or was someone clever or wise in how they approached the problem?		
Outcome	How did each story end? Did the story end in about the same way or differently?		

ANCHOR CHART 36: COMPARING SIMILARITIES AND DIFFERENCES BETWEEN INFORMATIONAL TEXTS

Source 1: _____

Source 2: _____

Fill in each box for both of your sources.

TEXT ELEMENTS	ANALYZING INFORMATIONAL ELEMENTS	SOURCE 1	SOURCE 2
Purpose	What is the purpose of the text? Does the source make the purpose clear? How is the purpose different in each text?		
Range and Depth of Information	Does the source contain information about the whole topic (like tornadoes), or does it focus on one part of the topic (like how to stay safe during a tornado)?		
Evidence	What kinds of details does the source provide to support the central idea: facts, examples, definitions, quotes, opinions, other?		
Point of View	Is the point of view of the author clear? Explain.		
Text Features	Does the source present information with headings, subheadings, and other informational text features or does it present the information in connected paragraphs without many text features?		
Graphics	Does the source include graphics? What kinds of graphics? How are they helpful?		

Domingo, the capital

...hair and my dad said in Spanish "careful

...right?" she asked back. I was laughing really hard because that

...The good thing is that no harsh feelings get caught in the action.

...the best for me, they want me to go to school and graduate with a

...regret studying. A regular basic phrase they repeat to me is

...monotony problems to us" something I can never contradict.

...hair stylist 6 days a week. She studied that on one of the best

...Dominican Republic at the time which was around 20 years

...'s a good thing. My dad is a sales man for a new company

...focus on high-quality windows that are tough enough to

...the ocean areas which are the most touristic-based

...I want, what I dream of, and no matter how big or

...them and to never let go because dreams are

...our dreams can become true makes us

...change, our dreams change too. My dad and I

...grew up. I was 14 at the time. He simply

...He looked at me and said "Fidel, I know.

...him the you-think-I'm-stupid look

..." I said. He took a deep breath and

...to achieve

...well on tests.

...I applaud him

...ports, and a social life. He

...at he had gotten accepted to almost

...our class with a 4.2 GPA. On the night

...students received scholarships for the

...ip he got was for $500. The night

...he wasn't going to get any mor...

Then, the final name was...

...rigues,

...en he

...deep

...recruitment.

...nickname but my...

...My parents are both

...my dear parents, I can't imagine to talk abo...

... expect to really perceive and classify Sánchez. T...

...protective. Without them I wouldn't be who I am toda...

...mother school completely shakes the earth...

...full they help me true again. They are th...

...They are the ones that ar...

PART III

Hands-on Support
for Responding
and Writing

CHAPTER 6

CUE CARDS FOR ORAL REHEARSAL

I used to be fond of saying, "If students can't *talk about it*, they won't be able to *write about it*," expecting that the reverse was also true: that talking about reading meant students could then write about it. But over the years, I've realized this was mostly wishful thinking. Even if students *can* talk about what they've read in a class discussion, that doesn't guarantee they'll be able to write about it.

Why is that? Maybe it was just an assumption because at some level it does make sense (talking about something and writing about it—isn't that pretty similar?). Apparently not! Written language (an answer or any other form of writing), is not simply "talk written down." A discussion affords speakers and listeners cues that are unavailable in written language—such as tone of voice, body language, word choice independent of correct spelling, more flexibility in sentence structure, and encouragement and affirmation from your audience.

By contrast, when you write, it's just you and a blank piece of paper (or empty screen). That's not enough to get some students to put pen to paper and keep going. They feel insecure: *What if what I write isn't good enough?* Some feel scared: *What will happen if I get this wrong?* The saddest part of this is that many students *do* know the answer, or at least know enough to make an attempt. But lack of confidence yields at best a half-hearted effort.

Oral Rehearsal Before Written Response

We saw in the virtual lesson that we can change this outcome with no more than an index card—a card that cued students' responses to a question orally with precisely the same language they would use to respond in writing. I call this oral rehearsal. As with any rehearsal, it's a practice session for the "big performance." In this case, the "performance" is the response in writing where students "publish" their thinking.

As noted in the virtual lesson, this instructional component is crazy simple. The cue card contains sentence starters. At this point, you've already discussed the text, so the card is just a bridge where students say out loud to a partner *exactly what they will write on their paper*, completing the prompts accordingly: *The central idea in _____ is _____. Here's how the author developed this central idea: _____.* They power through to the end of the response. I model the process first with one student, then listen in as student partners practice with each other. I offer support where needed, but happily, my services are seldom required.

If comprehension has been adequate, you can count on this step to propel students toward the goal: writing a well-constructed response. Cue cards for the oral rehearsal of responses to all questions in this book are provided in this section. It may be useful to copy these cards onto cardstock, or laminate them for durability.

Note that the cue cards can be photocopied from the book or downloaded and printed from https://wwnorton.com/AwesomeAnswers, for distribution to students.

CUE CARD FOR QUESTION I.1:
Which details are most surprising?

1. Something surprising in _____ was_____.
   TITLE OF SOURCE

2. This was surprising because _____.

3. Evidence that showed this is _____.

4. This is important because _____.*

*If there are other surprises, repeat steps 1-4 for each surprise

---

CUE CARD FOR QUESTION 1.2:

Which details were the most helpful in figuring out _____?

1. The detail that helped me most was _____.

2. This was the final clue I needed to figure out _____.

3. Some other clues that made sense with this were _____.

4. Some clues that were not very helpful were _____ because _____.

CUE CARD FOR QUESTION 2.1:

Paraphrase this [paragraph] to show its meaning in your own words.

1. Words I need to keep are: _____.

2. Words I can change but keep the same meaning are: _____.

3. Sentences or phrases I can combine are: _____.

4. Here is the way I would paraphrase this [paragraph]—using a different beginning than the one the author used: _____.

CUE CARD FOR QUESTION 2.2:

How does the author develop the idea of _____?

1. In _____, the author develops the idea of _____.
   NAME OF STORY OR SOURCE   STATE THE IDEA IDENTIFIED
                                                              IN THE QUESTION

2. The author developed this idea using these details:

   At first, _____.

   Then, _____.

   Finally, _____.

3. These details are important because they show _____.

CUE CARD FOR QUESTION 2.3:
What is the central idea/theme of _____ and how does the author develop it?

1. The central idea in _____ is _____.

2. The author developed this idea using these details:

   At first, _____.

   Then, _____.

   Finally, _____.

3. These details are important because they show _____.

CUE CARD FOR QUESTION 2.4:
What is the main idea of this [paragraph] and how does the author develop it?

1. The main idea in _____ is _____.

2. One piece of evidence from the text is _____.

3. Another piece of evidence from the text is _____.

4. Optional: A final piece of evidence is _____.

5. This issue is important to consider because _____.

1. At the <u>beginning</u> of the story, _____,
   WHERE WAS IT HAPPENING?
   _____ was having a problem. The problem was _____.
   CHARACTER

2. In the <u>middle</u> of the story, these things happened before the problem got solved:

   a. _____

   b. _____

   c. _____

3. At the <u>end</u> of the story, the problem got solved when _____
   and the story ended when _____.

CUE CARD FOR QUESTION 2.6:
What conclusion can you draw about [character, problem, etc.]?

1. One conclusion I can draw about _____ is _____.

2. A detail that supports this is _____.

3. Another detail that supports this is _____.

[If you can find other good details, add them here.]

4. This is important because _____.

CUE CARD FOR QUESTION 3.1:
What character trait (or feeling) does [character] mainly show in this story?

1. The character trait (or feeling) that this character mainly shows in this story (or in this part of the story) is _____.

2. One example of this trait (or feeling) in the story is when _____.

3. Here is a quote that shows this trait (or feeling): "_____."

4. Another example of this trait (or feeling) in the story is when _____.

5. Here is another quote that shows this trait (or feeling): "_____."

6. This trait (or feeling) is important to this character because _____.

CUE CARD FOR QUESTION 3.2:
What is the character's attitude, and how does it make a difference?

1. _____ attitude was _____.
   NAME OF CHARACTER

2. Evidence in the story that shows this is _____.

3. Something else that shows this is _____.

4. I think the character had this attitude because _____.

5. This attitude made a difference because _____.

CUE CARD FOR QUESTION 3.3:
What motivated [character] to _____?

1. This character was motivated by _____.

2. The problem the character was motivated to solve was _____.

3. Here's what happened when this character tried to solve his problem: _____.

4. This shows that the character _____.

5. Later in the story this character's motivation did/did not change. I know this because _____.

6. Here's what I learned about motivation from this story: _____.

CUE CARD FOR QUESTION 3.4:
What is the relationship between [Character A] and [Character B]?

1. In _____ , the characters did/did not have a
   <small>TITLE OF SOURCE</small>
   positive relationship.

2. I think the best way to describe this relationship is _____.

3. One detail that showed this relationship was _____.

4. Another detail that showed this relationship was _____.

5. The important thing to understand about this relationship is ____.

CUE CARD FOR QUESTION 3.5:
What is [Character's / Author's] point of view about _____?
How does the character (or author) show this?

1. In _____ , the character's/author's point of
   <small>TITLE OF SOURCE</small>
   view about _____was _____.

2. One detail that showed this point of view was _____.

3. Another detail that showed this point of view was _____.

4. The important thing to understand about this point of view is _____.

CUE CARD FOR QUESTION 3.6:
What are the most important differences between [Character A] and [Character B]?

1. In _____, one of the big differences

   between _____ and _____ is

               CHARACTER A   CHARACTER B

   _____.

2. A detail that shows this difference is _____.

3. Another important difference is _____.

4. A detail that shows this difference is _____.

5. These differences between the characters are important because ____.

CUE CARD FOR QUESTION 3.7:
What is the relationship between [the setting] and [the problem] in _____?

1. This story/event _____ took place _____.

                    WHAT IS THE WORD?

2. The problem was was _____.

3. The time and place were important to this situation because _____

   _____.

4. In another time and place this problem wouldn't have happened

   because _____.

CUE CARD FOR QUESTION 4.1:

What does [word] mean and what clue in the text helped you to understand it?

1. The word _____ means _____.
   <small>WHAT IS THE WORD?</small>

2. The clue in the text that helped me understand this was _____.

3. This clue helped me because _____.

CUE CARD FOR QUESTION 4.2:

What word might the author use to make the meaning in this [sentence] clearer?

1. I would change the word _____ to _____.
   <small>OLD WORD</small> <small>NEW WORD</small>

2. I think this is a more precise word because _____.

CUE CARD FOR QUESTION 4.3:

What words create the tone in this [paragraph]? What is the tone?

1. The author uses tone words to describe _____.

2. Some of these tone words are _____.

3. These words create a tone that is _____ because _____.

4. [Repeat steps 1–3 if there are other words that show a different tone.]

CUE CARD FOR QUESTION 4.4:

What author's craft (like description, dialogue, internal dialogue, and gesture) does the author use in this [part of the story] and why do you think the author included it?

1. A craft the author uses in this part of _____ is _____.
   TITLE OF SOURCE

2. Here is what is happening in this part of the [story]: _____.

3. One example of this craft is _____.

4. It shows _____.

5. Another example of this craft is: _____.

6. It shows _____.

7. [If there are more examples, repeat both the example and what it shows.]

8. I think the author used this craft because _____.

CUE CARD FOR QUESTION 4.5:

What figurative language (like simile, metaphor, personification, idiom, or hyperbole) does the author use in this [paragraph] and why do you think the author chose it?

1. One kind of figurative language in _____ is _____.
   TITLE OF SOURCE

2. One example of this is _____.

3. Another example of this is _____.

4. [Add more examples if you can find them.]

5. [If you can find another kind of figurative language, repeat steps 1–3.]

6. I think the author chose to use this figurative language because ____.

CUE CARD FOR QUESTION 4.6:

What elements of a [fable] did you find in this text? Find at least two elements and explain how the author uses them.

1. _____ has lots of elements of a _____.
   TITLE OF SOURCE   FABLE OR OTHER GENRE

2. One element is _____.

3. Here is what happens that shows this: _____.

4. Another element of this genre that I see in this text is _____.

5. Here is an example that shows this: _____.

6. This is an important genre because _____.

1. I think the author wrote this poem to show his feelings about _____.

2. That feeling is _____.

3. One example of how language makes this feeling stand out is _____.

4. Another example that shows how the poet uses language is _____.

5. The look and sound of this writing adds to the feeling because ___.

6. When you put the look, sound, and language of this poem together it makes me feel _____ because _____.

1. The text feature is _____.

2. It shows _____.

3. An important detail about this is _____.

4. I think the author included this text feature because _____.

CUE CARD FOR QUESTION 5.2:

What text structure did the author choose for writing [about this topic] and what is the most likely reason the author chose it?

1. The structure of this text is _____.

2. I know this because _____.

3. An example from the text that shows this structure is _____.

4. Another text example that shows this structure is _____.

5. I think the author chose this structure to write about this topic because _____.

CUE CARD FOR QUESTION 5.3:

What kind of information does the author provide in [paragraph A] and why does the author include it?

1. The kind of information the author is providing in _____ is _____.

2. I know this because _____.

3. One example is _____.

4. Another example is _____.

5. I think the author chose to put this information right here because _____.

CUE CARD FOR QUESTION 5.4:

How does [paragraph A] connect to [paragraph B]?

1. [Paragraph A] that begins _____ is connected to [Paragraph B] that begins _____ by _____.

2. In the first [paragraph] the author says _____.

3. In the next [paragraph] the author says _____.

4. This was/was not a good way to connect these paragraphs because _____.

CUE CARD FOR QUESTION 5.5:

Why did the author choose to begin/end the story with this [paragraph]?

1. The author begins (ends) this story by _____.

2. Here is a detail that shows this: _____.

3. Something else the author does at the beginning (end) of the story is _____.

4. Here is a detail that shows this: _____.

5. I think this was/was not a good way to begin (end) this story because _____.

CUE CARD FOR QUESTION 5.6:

Where is the flashback in the story and why did
the author most likely include it?

1. There is a flashback in this story when _____.

2. The flashback shows that in the past_____.

3. Here is one example from the flashback: _____.

4. Here is another example from the flashback: _____.

5. It was important for the author to include the flashback because ____.

CUE CARD FOR QUESTION 5.7:

What is the backstory for this [story], and why
did the author most likely include it?

1. The main part of this story is about _____.

2. There is a backstory at the beginning/end about _____.

3. The backstory explains _____.

4. The author probably included this backstory because _____.

5. I think it is important to understand this because _____.

CUE CARD FOR QUESTION 5.8:

Why do you think the author included this quote from another author at the beginning of this [chapter]?

1. I think the author included this quote to show _____.

2. The quote explains _____.

3. Some examples from the text that show this are _____.

4. I think it was important to include this quote because _____.

CUE CARD FOR QUESTION 6.1:

How would this story change if it were told from [new narrator's] point of view?

1. If this story was written from _____'s point of view, it
   DIFFERENT CHARACTER'S
   would be different because you could see this character's motivation, attitude, and feelings more clearly:

2. For motivation you would see _____ based on this detail in the
   text:_____.

3. For attitude you would see _____ based on this detail in the text: _____.

4. For feelings you would see _____ based on this detail in the text: ___.

5. It would be good to tell this story from the character's point of
   view because _____.

CUE CARD FOR QUESTION 6.2:

What is your point of view about _____, and how is it the same or different from the point of view of the author?

1. My point of view about _____ is _____.

2. The main reason I support this position is _____.

3. Some evidence that supports this reason is _____.

4. Another reason for my position is _____.

5. Some evidence that supports this reason is _____.

[If there are more reasons and evidence, explain them here.]

6. Some people disagree and think that _____.

7. I think they are wrong because _____.

8. We need to find a solution to this problem because _____.

CUE CARD FOR QUESTION 6.3:
What was the author's purpose for including this [paragraph/sentence]?

1. The purpose of this paragraph/sentence is _____.

2. Here are some details that show this: _____.

3. I think the author included this information because _____.

CUE CARD FOR QUESTION 7.1:
How did this video add to your understanding of _____?

1. This video, _____, told about _____.

2. Here is what happened: _____.

3. The message is _____.

4. Some of the images and other features of the video that added meaning to this message were _____.

5. These images and features were powerful because _____.

6. Overall, I think this video worked well (or didn't work well) as a text because _____.

CUE CARD FOR QUESTION 7.2:
Why do you think the author included this illustration (or photograph)?

1. The photograph (or illustration) I'm describing is _____.

2. It shows _____.

3. This photograph (or illustration) makes me feel _____ because _____.

4. I think the author included this photograph (or illustration) because _____.

5. Something I figured by looking at this photograph (or illustration) that wasn't in the print text that goes with this picture is _____.

6. A question I still have is _____.

CUE CARD FOR QUESTION 8.1:

Which details from [the text] are relevant to the argument that _____?

1. The [article] _____ includes information about ____.

2. One relevant detail that support this is _____.

3. Another relevant detail that supports this is _____.

4. [If you can find other relevant evidence]: Another detail that supports this is_____.

5. It is important to understand _____ because _____.

CUE CARD FOR QUESTION 8.2:

What additional evidence for _____ could the author have included to make the argument more convincing?

1. In _____, the author provides evidence showing _____.
   TITLE OF SOURCE

2. For example, _____.

3. Another kind of evidence the author could have included is _____ because _____.

4. The author also could have included evidence such as _____ because _____.

5. It could be important to include additional evidence because _____.

Which source does a better job of explaining _____?
Cite specific evidence to support your answer.

1. The source that did a better job of explaining _____
   WHAT WAS BEING EXPLAINED?

   was _____.
   TITLE

2. This explanation was clearer because_____.

3. Here is an example: _____.

4. By contrast, _____ the explanation was not as clear
   TITLE OF WEAKER SOURCE

   because _____.

5. An example that shows this is _____.

6. This difference is important because _____.

Here is what I would include in an answer that uses *both* sources:

1. The big idea, which is _____.

2. <u>Words</u> defined or explained in Source 1: _____ and in Source 2: _____.

3. <u>Facts</u> in Source 1: _____ and facts in Source 2: _____.

4. Important <u>quotes</u> from Source 1: _____ and from Source 2: _____.

5. A <u>story</u> from Source 1: _____ and from Source 2: _____.

6. A conclusion about the importance of the topic _____.

CUE CARD FOR QUESTION 9.3:

Use the information from these [two] sources to write a diary entry from your point of view, imagining that you are personally experiencing the situation identified in these sources. Be sure to include details from the informational sources you read.

1. Today's date is _____.

2. Here is what has been happening in my life recently: _____.

3. This makes me feel _____ because _____.

4. In my opinion, _____.

5. Your friend, _____.

CUE CARD FOR QUESTION 9.4:

Identify the central idea in Source #1 and Source #2. Then compare and contrast the way the author develops the central idea in each of the sources.

1. The [central idea] of both stories is _____.

2. Something important about the similarity and difference between these stories is _____.

3. In [Source #1], the author showed this central idea with these events: _____.

4. In [Source #2], the author showed this central idea with these events: _____.

5. This [central idea] is important because _____.

CHAPTER 7

SAMPLE CONSTRUCTED RESPONSES

Due to time constraints, I did not work with students to analyze a sample response in my virtual lesson described in Chapter 1. But this is an especially helpful step for visual learners who need to *see* something before they can do it themselves, or for students who need one more round of support before embarking on their own written answer. In this section I provide two models. The first is a full-score response that contains all the elements specified in the cue card sentence starters. The second response is one that would receive a partial score because it is missing essential pieces or is inaccurate in one or more ways. For the partial-score responses, there is a brief analysis at the end of this chapter explaining why the answer missed the mark.

If you choose to use both responses as teaching tools, deconstruct the full-score response first. Go through the response sentence by sentence, showing how it aligns with the criteria for a good answer. In another lesson, deconstruct the partial-score response in a similar fashion, this time making sure students recognize what is missing. What would they add to this answer to improve it? After you have worked through a few of these samples together, some students may be able to complete the analysis of additional samples independently and revise the partial-score response to meet the required criteria.

The texts in this chapter were selected to meet the needs of a range of grade levels. But if some samples don't meet your students' needs, choose a different text and create a more appropriate example yourself. You'll want to establish as solid a foundation as possible about what a good response looks like before moving on to the final step: where students write their own answer to a comprehension question.

Note that the sample responses can be photocopied from the book or downloaded and printed from https://wwnorton.com/AwesomeAnswers, for distribution to students.

Which details are most surprising?

Sample Question

Which details are the most surprising in the poem "The New Kid on the Block" by Jack Prelutsky?

Source: *The New Kid on the Block* by Jack Prelutsky (book of poems)

SAMPLE RESPONSE (FULL SCORE): WHY DOES THIS RESPONSE EARN A FULL SCORE?

Something surprising in the poem "The New Kid on the Block" is the detail in the last line that the new kid turns out to be a girl, when through the whole poem you probably thought it was a boy. Lots of evidence leads you to this conclusion. The new kid is tough and punches hard. The new kid has lots of muscles and likes to fight. The new kid picks on the guys. When I think of kids who act like this, I think of boys, which is why the detail at the end was so surprising. But this author teaches an important lesson here. Girls can act this way, too. Don't make a quick judgment before you know all the facts.

SAMPLE RESPONSE (PARTIAL SCORE): HOW COULD WE REVISE THIS FOR A FULL SCORE?

Something surprising in the poem "The New Kid on the Block" is that the new kid is a girl, not a boy like you expected. The girl did a lot of bad things like punching. The lesson is that girls should never act this way.

Which details were the most helpful in figuring out _____?

Sample Question

What details were the most helpful in figuring out the identity of the stranger in the book *The Stranger*?

Source: *The Stranger* by Chris Van Allsburg (picture book)

SAMPLE RESPONSE (FULL SCORE): WHY DOES THIS RESPONSE EARN A FULL SCORE?

The detail that helped me most to figure out who the stranger was in the book *The Stranger* was on the last page where the author says that the words "See you next fall" were etched in frost on the windows. I finally figured out the stranger was Jack Frost. Other clues from the beginning of the story got me thinking that the stranger had something to do with being cold. For example, the mercury in the thermometer was stuck at the bottom. There was a cold draft when the stranger was in the room. The leaf turned from green to red when he blew on it. These clues all fit together with the detail about the frost on the window. Other clues that were not as helpful were that the man didn't talk and he didn't know how to use a spoon because they didn't have anything to do with being cold.

SAMPLE RESPONSE (PARTIAL SCORE): HOW COULD WE REVISE THIS FOR A FULL SCORE?

I figured out that the stranger was Jack Frost. Some clues I used were that he wore old leather clothes. He didn't talk, and he never got sweaty when he worked. Then at the end, he wrote in frost on the window.

Paraphrase this [paragraph] to show its meaning in your own words.

Sample Question

Paraphrase the first stanza in the poem "The Land of Nod" by Robert Louis Stevenson:

From breakfast on through all the day
At home among my friends I stay,
But every night I go abroad
Afar into the Land of Nod.

Source: *A Child's Garden of Verses* by Robert Louis Stevenson (book of poems available online from Project Gutenburg)

SAMPLE RESPONSE (FULL SCORE):
WHY DOES THIS RESPONSE EARN A FULL SCORE?

All day long beginning at breakfast, I stay home with my friends. But at night I go far away across the sea to the Land of Nod.

SAMPLE RESPONSE (PARTIAL SCORE):
HOW COULD WE REVISE THIS FOR A FULL SCORE?

I stay home during the day and go far away at night.

How does the author develop the idea of _____?

SAMPLE RESPONSE (FULL SCORE): WHY DOES THIS RESPONSE EARN A FULL SCORE?

In "A Chance for Freedom," the author develops the idea of hope for the future for Young Hoon and Young Jun, two brothers who escaped North Korea for South Korea. Their life in North Korea had been very difficult. North Korea is very poor, and many people starve to death. They lived in huts there. To get to South Korea, they had to travel through China which was dangerous because they would have been punished or killed if the police found them. But the difficult journey was worth it because South Korea is so much better, and now they live with hope, not fear. They live in an apartment and eat well. They have hope for their future, getting an education, good jobs, and visiting America. These brothers show how important it is not to lose hope. With hope and effort, they got past very bad times and now have a better future.

SAMPLE RESPONSE (PARTIAL SCORE): HOW COULD WE REVISE THIS FOR A FULL SCORE?

In "A Chance for Freedom," two brothers lived in North Korea and they had no freedom. They finally got to South Korea and have hope because they go to school and can come to America. They had no freedom before, but now they do.

What is the central idea/theme of _____ and how does the author develop it?

Sample Question

What is the central idea/theme of the fable "The Bees and Wasps, and the Hornet" and how does the author develop it?

Source: "The Bees and Wasps, and the Hornet" by Aesop (fable available online from Project Gutenburg)

SAMPLE RESPONSE (FULL SCORE): WHY DOES THIS RESPONSE EARN A FULL SCORE?

The central idea of the fable "The Bees and Wasps, and the Hornet" is that if you say you can do something, you should be able to prove it. In this story, honey was found in a tree and both the Bees and the Wasps claimed it was theirs. They tried to let a judge decide, but the evidence wasn't that helpful. Witnesses had seen buzzing winged creatures that were black and yellow, which is true for wasps and bees. When someone suggested building a honeycomb to prove the case, the Wasps couldn't do it. In life, if you say you're good at something (like soccer or art), don't just talk about it. Demonstrate!

SAMPLE RESPONSE (PARTIAL SCORE): HOW COULD WE REVISE THIS FOR A FULL SCORE?

The central idea in the fable "The Bees and Wasps, and the Hornet" is that Bees make honey, not Wasps. There was an argument in this story about who really made the honey. It even went to court. That didn't prove anything. But the Bees could build a honeycomb.

What is the main idea of this [paragraph] and how does the author develop it?

Sample Question

What is the main idea under the heading "E-day Now, Play Later" in "News Debate: Snowed Out!" and how does the author develop it?

Source: "News Debate: Snowed Out!" (article available online from ReadWorks)

SAMPLE RESPONSE (FULL SCORE): WHY DOES THIS RESPONSE EARN A FULL SCORE?

The main idea in "E-day Now, Play Later" in "Snowed Out!" is that having online work on a day when school is canceled for snow is better than making up the day later. The author gives a few reasons for this. First, you already planned on having schoolwork. One student agreed: "A couple of hours of online work beats going in for additional days in June." Another reason is that if you have to do extra days in June, it could interfere with your family vacation. Also, if your school isn't air conditioned, you will be sweating. This issue may not matter to kids who live where it doesn't snow, but it matters a lot in states that get winter storms. I wish my town would think about this. And I bet the teachers would like E-days, too.

SAMPLE RESPONSE (PARTIAL SCORE): HOW COULD WE REVISE THIS FOR A FULL SCORE?

I think E-days are a great idea when it snows because you're not really going to school, but the time you spend on your work counts as school time. Then you don't have to make up the day when the weather gets hot and you want to be outside playing. Please vote for E-days.

Briefly summarize this story including only the key points.

Sample Question

Briefly summarize the story "Spaghetti" including only the key points.

Source: *Every Living Thing* by Cynthia Rylant (book of short stories)

SAMPLE RESPONSE (FULL SCORE):
WHY DOES THIS RESPONSE EARN A FULL SCORE?

Gabriel was outside, feeling very alone one night, wishing for some company. He heard a weak cry and at first he thought it might be the wind, but he heard it again, and went looking. That's when he saw a small gray kitten. Gabriel picked the kitten up and he smelled like pasta noodles, so he named it Spaghetti. He didn't feel so alone anymore and took Spaghetti home to show him where they would both live together. Even a kitten can be a very good friend and make your heart feel happy.

SAMPLE RESPONSE (PARTIAL SCORE):
HOW COULD WE REVISE THIS FOR A FULL SCORE?

Gabriel was outside and he was lonely. Finally, he found a cat and he named him Spaghetti. He liked Spaghetti a lot and he took him home.

What conclusion can you draw about [character, problem, etc.]?

Sample Question

What conclusion can you draw about Molly Pitcher in the poem "Molly Pitcher"?

Source: "Molly Pitcher" by Kate Brownlee Sherwood (poem available online from Project Gutenburg)

SAMPLE RESPONSE (FULL SCORE): WHY DOES THIS RESPONSE EARN A FULL SCORE?

One conclusion I can draw about Molly Pitcher in the poem "Molly Pitcher" is that she had a lot of courage and she was a hero. She was on the battlefield during the Battle of Monmouth and saw her husband get shot. Rather than crying and running off, she fired her husband's cannon: "Fired as she saw her husband do." George Washington told her she saved the day and the other soldiers cheered. I think this is important because Molly showed she could have just as much courage as any soldier on the battlefield. It didn't matter that she was a woman.

SAMPLE RESPONSE (PARTIAL SCORE): HOW COULD WE REVISE THIS FOR A FULL SCORE?

One conclusion I can draw about Molly Pitcher was she fought in the Battle of Monmouth. She fired her husband's cannon when he got shot. Later everyone cheered, even George Washington. The Yankees won and the British lost.

What character trait (or feeling) does [character] mainly show in this story?

Sample Question

In the fable "Mercury and the Woodman," what character trait does the Woodman mainly show?

Source: "Mercury and the Woodman" by Aesop (fable available online from Project Gutenburg)

SAMPLE RESPONSE (FULL SCORE): WHY WOULD THIS RECEIVE A FULL SCORE?

The main character trait that the Woodman shows in this fable is honesty. He is honest when Mercury first dove into the pool and brought up a golden axe. The Woodman said, "No, that is not my axe," although he was poor and would love an axe made of gold. Then Mercury dove down again and brought up a silver axe. But the Woodman declared again that his axe was just an ordinary one with a wooden handle. This trait of honesty is important to the Woodman because he chose to tell the truth when he could have lied and gotten rich. It shows he is a good and truthful person.

SAMPLE RESPONSE (PARTIAL SCORE): HOW COULD WE REVISE THIS FOR A FULL SCORE?

In "Mercury and the Woodman," the Woodman was always honest. He lost his axe but he didn't lie about it. This happened many times when Mercury asked if the axe was his and he never lied about it. His real axe was made of wood.

What is the character's attitude, and how does it make a difference?

Sample Question

In the story *Hey, Little Ant*, what was the boy's attitude toward the ant and how does it make a difference?

Source: *Hey, Little Ant* by Hannah Hoose and Phillip Hoose (picture book)

SAMPLE RESPONSE (FULL SCORE): WHY WOULD THIS RECEIVE A FULL SCORE?

In *Hey, Little Ant,* the boy's attitude was he thought he was superior. He thought he was superior to the ant and he showed this in lots of the things he said. For example, he said he was big, and the ant was small, so he could squish him quickly if he wanted to. He said the ant was just a "speck" that ran around. He didn't have a family (like the boy did) and he and his friends think its fun to squish ants. Even when the ant tried to explain that he did have a family and his family needed him, the boy didn't care. You can't really tell why the boy had this attitude, but maybe sometime someone treated him like *he* didn't matter. The boy's attitude makes a difference because at the end of the story you're not sure if he still plans to step on the ant. This would kill the little ant.

SAMPLE RESPONSE (PARTIAL SCORE): HOW COULD WE REVISE THIS FOR A FULL SCORE?

The boy's attitude is self-centered. All he thinks about is himself. He wants to step on the ant because he's bigger and stronger, and he doesn't care how the ant feels about this. He needs to think more about other creatures, even if they are small.

What motivated [character] to _____?

Sample Question

In the poem "The Ballad of Birmingham," what motivated the daughter to want to join the Freedom March?

Source: "The Ballad of Birmingham" by Dudley Randall (poem available online)

SAMPLE RESPONSE (FULL SCORE): WHY WOULD THIS RECEIVE A FULL SCORE?

The daughter in this poem valued justice and that is what motivated her to want to join the Freedom March. This took place during Civil Rights, when Martin Luther King Jr. was alive, and black people didn't have the same freedom as white people. She said she wanted to "march the streets of Birmingham to make our country free." Her mother said she couldn't go because it was too dangerous. Instead she could go to church because it was safe there. But it wasn't safe. A bomb went off in the church and the girl was killed. She died for freedom. What a terrible tragedy! A church should be a peaceful place, not a place for violence.

SAMPLE RESPONSE (PARTIAL SCORE): HOW COULD WE REVISE THIS FOR A FULL SCORE?

In "The Ballad of Birmingham," the daughter wanted to join the Freedom March because she would be safe. But she wasn't safe because she went to church and there was a bomb that exploded, and she got killed.

What is the relationship between [Character A] and [Character B]?

Sample Question

In the story "Best Friends," what was the relationship between the narrator and her best friend, Ann?

Source: "Best Friends" by Mary Beth Olson (short story available in *Chicken Soup for the Kid's Soul*)

SAMPLE RESPONSE (FULL SCORE):
WHY WOULD THIS RECEIVE A FULL SCORE?

In the story "Best Friends," the narrator did not have a good relationship with her friend Ann. She thought they were best friends, but when Ann came over to play, she said she would stay only if her friend gave her the miniature moccasins she saw on a table. The narrator's aunt who died had given her those moccasins so they were special. But she gave them to Ann because she really wanted a playmate. Later she realized she had made a big mistake and she cried. The next day she asked for the moccasins back. Ann returned them, but she was mean about it. "I didn't like them anyway." After that, the girls stopped being friends. The narrator learned an important lesson here because real friends want to be with you because they like you, not because you give them things. They don't take advantage of you.

SAMPLE RESPONSES (PARTIAL SCORE):
HOW COULD WE REVISE THIS FOR A FULL SCORE?

The narrator and Ann didn't have a good relationship. Ann was mean to her when she came to play and made the girl give her some toy moccasins. The narrator should have defended herself, but she didn't. Finally, she got the moccasins back. The narrator learned that Ann was not a good friend.

What is [Character's/Author's] point of view about _____? How does the character (or author) show this?

Sample Question

In Lou Gehrig's "Farewell to Baseball Address," what is Lou's point of view about leaving the sport that he loved? How does he show this?

Source: "Farewell to Baseball Address" by Lou Gehrig (speech available online)

SAMPLE RESPONSE (FULL SCORE):
WHY WOULD THIS RECEIVE FULL SCORE?

In Lou Gehrig's "Farewell to Baseball Address," his point of view was that he was a very lucky man even though he was sick and had to leave the sport he loved. In fact, he says he is the "luckiest man on the face of the earth." This is surprising because people don't usually feel lucky when they get really sick. But Lou Gehrig shows what he means. He was lucky to meet great people like Ed Barrow, Jacob Ruppert, and Miller Huggins. He was lucky to have thousands of fans who loved him and he won a lot of trophies. I think Lou Gehrig's point of view is important because it shows that even when you get a bad break in life, you should remember that good things have happened in your life, too. That's what Lou Gehrig did, and I hope I'd be like that, too.

SAMPLE RESPONSE (PARTIAL SCORE):
HOW COULD WE REVISE THIS FOR A FULL SCORE?

In Lou Gehrig's "Farewell to Baseball Address," Lou's point of view was he felt lucky. He was really happy he had a chance to play baseball for many years. Lots of good things happened to him. Then he got sick and he couldn't play anymore.

What are the most important differences between [Character A] and [Character B]?

Sample Question

In "Some Pig," the first chapter in *Charlotte's Web*, what are the most important differences between Fern and her father, Mr. Arable?

Source: *Charlotte's Web* by E.B. White (novel)

SAMPLE RESPONSE (FULL SCORE): WHY DOES THIS RESPONSE EARN A FULL SCORE?

In "Some Pig," one of the big differences between Fern and her father, Mr. Arable, was they had different goals. Fern wanted to keep Wilbur, the pig, and Mr. Arable wanted to sell him. When Wilbur was five weeks old, Mr. Arable said he was big enough to sell. Fern wanted to keep Wilbur. That was because she loved him. Wilbur even waited at the bus stop with her. And he followed her into her house. But Mr. Arable's feelings were different. Wilbur was getting expensive to feed. "Mr. Arable was not willing to provide for him any longer." In the end, Wilbur went to live in her uncle's barn. That way, she could visit him. Although these characters had different goals and feelings, the important thing is they made a plan that worked for both of them. They compromised.

SAMPLE RESPONSE (PARTIAL SCORE): HOW COULD WE REVISE THIS FOR A FULL SCORE?

Fern and her father had different feelings about Wilbur the pig. Fern really loved him. She treated him like one of her dolls. But Mr. Arable didn't like pigs and he wanted to get rid of him. He sold Wilbur. It was his choice because he's the dad.

What is the relationship between [the setting] and [the problem] in _____?

Sample Question

What is the relationship between the setting and the problem in the story *Unstoppable*?

Source: *Unstoppable: How Jim Thorpe and the Carlisle Indian School Football Team Defeated Army* by Art Colson (picture book)

SAMPLE RESPONSE (FULL SCORE): WHY DOES THIS RESPONSE EARN A FULL SCORE?

In the story *Unstoppable*, the setting was a boarding school for Indians about the year 1900. Jim Thorpe, an American Indian, was sent to this school so they could teach him *not* to be an Indian and more like other American kids. "The schools cut the children's hair and burned their traditional clothes." They wouldn't allow them to speak their Indian language and they beat them if they did. Back then, some people thought it was okay to treat Indians like this. If Jim Thorpe was a boy today, he wouldn't have to suffer at a school like this. Although today there is still prejudice and discrimination against Indians and other races, it is not as bad as this. There are no more Indian boarding schools. Everyone should read this book to understand how Indians have suffered in America.

SAMPLE RESPONSE (PARTIAL SCORE): HOW COULD WE REVISE THIS FOR A FULL SCORE?

Jim Thorpe had a different name before he went to a school for Indians where they changed his name and were mean to him. But he did learn to play football there. He became a great player. I don't think we have Indian schools anymore, which is a good thing. The setting was good for football, but bad for Indians.

What does [word] mean and what clue in the text helped you to understand it?

Sample Question

What does <u>moored</u> mean in stanza 4 of Robert Louis Stevenson's poem "Block City": *This one is sailing and that one is moored*?

Source: "Block City" by Robert Louis Stevenson (poem available online from Project Gutenburg)

SAMPLE RESPONSE (FULL SCORE): WHY WOULD THIS RECEIVE A FULL SCORE?

In "Block City," <u>moored</u> means not sailing, like the boat is tied up at the dock. The poem says, "This one is sailing and that one is moored," so it seems like it would be the opposite of sailing.

SAMPLE RESPONSE (PARTIAL SCORE): HOW COULD WE REVISE THIS FOR A FULL SCORE?

I think <u>moored</u> means that the sailors are on the ship because the next line says, "Hark to the song of the sailors aboard!"

What word might the author use to make the meaning in this [sentence] clearer?

Sample Question

What word might the author use instead of *walked* to make the meaning in these paragraphs clearer?

> *Lucy got off the school bus and <u>walked</u> up the driveway toward her house. Her report card was in her backpack and she could hardly wait to show her mother.*

> *Lucy got off the school bus and <u>walked</u> up the driveway toward her house. Her report card was in her backpack and she was worried about what her mother might say.*

Source: Use student writing samples with names removed, short paragraphs that you write yourself, or the sample I wrote and included in the question above.

SAMPLE RESPONSE (FULL SCORE): WHY WOULD THIS RECEIVE A FULL SCORE?

For the first paragraph, I would change the word *walked* to *raced*. I think that's a more precise word because if she wanted to show her report card to her mom, it must have been a good one. She would want to get to her house quickly.

For the second paragraph, I would change *walked* to *trudged*, which is a more precise word. Since Lucy was worried about showing her report card to her mom, she probably didn't get very good grades so she wouldn't want to get to her house any sooner than necessary. She would walk slowly.

SAMPLE RESPONSE (PARTIAL SCORE): HOW COULD WE REVISE THIS FOR A FULL SCORE?

I would change the word *walked* in these paragraphs to *hiked*. Maybe the driveway was long and steep, and that word gives you a better picture in your mind.

What words create the tone in this [paragraph]? What is the tone?

Sample Question

What words create the tone in the first two paragraphs of *Heidi*, Chapter 1: Up the Mountain to Alm-Uncle? What is the tone?

Source: *Heidi* by Johanna Spyri (novel available online from Project Gutenburg)

SAMPLE RESPONSE (FULL SCORE): WHY WOULD THIS RECEIVE A FULL SCORE?

Some of the words that create the tone in the first paragraphs of *Heidi* describe the setting: "green and shady meadow," "fragrance of the short grass," "sturdy mountain-plants," "clear sunny morning in June." These are happy images and make the tone seem hopeful. The author also talks about the little girl and says, "her little cheeks were aglow." She had "small feet shod in thick, nailed mountain-shoes," and she "slowly and laboriously plodded its way up in the heat." These words let you know the little girl was poor and walking in the heat was hard. I think the author is showing a tone that is hopeful, even though life is difficult.

SAMPLE RESPONSE (PARTIAL SCORE): HOW COULD WE REVISE THIS FOR A FULL SCORE?

I think the tone is friendly. The author describes the people by saying, "the wayfarers met with greetings from all sides." Friendly people would greet you like this, so that is why I think the tone is friendly.

What author's craft (like description, dialogue, internal dialogue, and gesture) does the author use in this [part of the story] and why do you think the author included it?

Sample Question

Choose one craft (description, dialogue, internal dialogue, or gesture) that the author uses in the excerpt from *Peter Pan*, Chapter 3. Why do you think the author included this craft?

Source: *Peter Pan* by J.M. Barrie (novel available online from Project Gutenburg)

SAMPLE RESPONSE (FULL SCORE): WHY WOULD THIS RECEIVE A FULL SCORE?

One craft that the author used in this excerpt from *Peter Pan* is dialogue. In this part of the story, Peter has just come to Wendy's house looking for his shadow. There is a lot of dialogue because they start talking to each other. First, Wendy is nice and asks, "Boy, why are you crying?" Peter asks Wendy her name and she answers, "Wendy Moira Angela Darling," and then asks Peter his name. He says, "Peter Pan." Wendy thinks that's a very short name, which makes Peter angry. But then it gets worse when Wendy asks Peter's address and he says, "Second to the right and then straight on till morning." Wendy tells him, "What a funny address." I think the author included this dialogue to show that Peter and Wendy didn't get off to a very good start with their friendship. Also, Wendy seems confident and acts like she's better than Peter.

SAMPLE RESPONSE (PARTIAL SCORE): HOW COULD WE REVISE THIS FOR A FULL SCORE?

One craft the author uses in this part of the story is gestures. Peter and Wendy are just getting to know each other and the gestures and small actions show how Peter is feeling. First, when he tried to stick his shadow back on, he <u>shuddered</u>. This shows he was upset. He <u>bowed</u> when he introduced himself to Wendy, which shows he was polite. Later, Peter <u>gulped</u> when Wendy thought he had a shortish name. He seems a little scared of Wendy.

What figurative language (like simile, metaphor, personification, idiom, or hyperbole) does the author use in this [paragraph] and why do you think the author chose it?

Sample Question

What figurative language (like simile, metaphor, personification, idiom, or hyperbole) does the author use in the poem "The Wind and the Leaves" and why do you think the author chose it?

Source: "The Wind and the Leaves" by George Cooper (poem available online from Project Gutenburg)

SAMPLE RESPONSE (FULL SCORE): WHY WOULD THIS RECEIVE A FULL SCORE?

The poet George Cooper uses a lot of personification in his poem "The Wind and the Leaves." In Stanza 1 he invites the leaves to come and <u>play</u> and to put on their <u>dress</u> of red and gold. (Leaves don't really play and they don't wear dresses.) In Stanza 2 the leaves <u>dance</u> and <u>sing</u> and in Stanza 3 the brook <u>sings</u> a farewell song. (Things in nature like leaves and brooks don't dance and sing.) In the last stanza, the winter <u>called</u> to the leaves. (Of course, winter doesn't actually call.) I think this poet chose personification because it makes the leaves seem like they are alive and you can really picture the scene in your mind where all these actions are happening.

SAMPLE RESPONSE (PARTIAL SCORE): HOW COULD WE REVISE THIS FOR A FULL SCORE?

The poet George Cooper used personification to show that the leaves and wind were acting like people. It was getting to be winter and the leaves fell off the trees and disappeared. They talked to the lambs and the crickets. At the end the leaves were hiding under the snow.

What elements of a [fable] did you find in this text? Find at least two elements and explain how the author uses them.

Sample Question

What elements of a fable did you find in "The Old Lion and the Fox"? Find at least two elements and explain how the author uses them.

Source: "The Old Lion and the Fox" by Aesop (fable available online from Project Gutenburg)

SAMPLE RESPONSE (FULL SCORE):
WHY WOULD THIS RECEIVE A FULL SCORE?

In "The Old Lion and the Fox," there are many elements of a fable. First, there are two characters and they are both animals, but they talk and act like real people. Here is what happens: The old Lion says he's sick and invites the Fox to come into his cave. This is a trick because other friends have come to visit, but the Lion eats them. The Fox notices that footsteps go *into* the cave, but no footsteps come *out*. Fox says he's not going inside. This is another element of a fable, that the good character survives because of some important trait: He is clever. A third element of a fable is that there is a moral. In this story the moral is to learn from other people's mistakes, so the same bad thing won't happen to you. Fables are important because you can learn the same lesson as the characters. In this fable you can learn to look for warning signs to stay out of trouble.

SAMPLE RESPONSE (PARTIAL SCORE):
HOW COULD WE REVISE THIS FOR A FULL SCORE?

"The Old Lion and the Fox" is a fable. It has talking animals and the Lion learns a lesson. The Lion invites the Fox into his cave, but the Fox won't go inside. The Lion learns a lesson not to eat his friends. Fables always teach a lesson.

Why do you think the author wrote this as a [poem]?

Sample Question

Why do you think the author wrote "October's Party" as a poem?

Source: "October's Party" by George Cooper (poem available online from Project Gutenburg)

SAMPLE RESPONSE (FULL SCORE):
WHY WOULD THIS RECEIVE A FULL SCORE?

I think the author wrote "October's Party" as a poem because he wanted to share his feelings about how great this month is. He uses language to show these feelings. Sometimes he uses personification like "October gave a party;" and "The Sunshine spread a carpet." You can picture these images with a simile like "The sight was like a rainbow." Also, there are words like crimson, scarlet, and fluttered. This poem even sounds happy when you read it out loud. There are short lines, and it rhymes and has a nice rhythm. By writing about October as a poem it feels like a song in my head. The author creates so many beautiful images that it makes me love October, too.

SAMPLE RESPONSE (PARTIAL SCORE):
HOW COULD WE REVISE THIS FOR A FULL SCORE?

The main feeling in "October's Party" is happiness. October is like a party with leaves, sunshine, and wind. The words make it sound like everyone is having a good time. Something else that makes this a poem is that it rhymes. Also, there are stanzas. This poem makes me want to have a party in October.

What is this text feature and what is the most likely reason the author included it?

Sample Question

What is this text feature in "China Today—China's Population" and what is the most likely reason the author included it?

Source: "China Today—China's Population" (article available online from ReadWorks)

SAMPLE RESPONSE (FULL SCORE): WHY WOULD THIS RECEIVE A FULL SCORE?

The text feature in "China Today—China's Population" is a graph. It shows the number of people living in China compared to the number of people living in the United States. There are more than 1,300,000,000 people in China compared to just over 300,000,000 in the United States. I think the author included a graph with this information because although it tells in the article that there are four times more people in China than in the U.S., the graph shows more visibly what this means. The bar for China's population is four times as tall as the bar for the U.S. This is even more amazing because both countries are about the same size.

SAMPLE RESPONSE (PARTIAL SCORE): HOW COULD WE REVISE THIS FOR A FULL SCORE?

The text feature in "China Today—China's Population" is a graph. It shows the number of people living in China compared to the number of people living in the United States. There are a lot more people in China. I think the author included a graph to show there are more people in China than in the U.S.

What text structure did the author choose for writing [about this topic] and what is the most likely reason the author chose it?

Sample Question

What text structure did the author choose for writing "News Debate: Cash Courses," and what is the most likely reason the author chose it?

Source: "News Debate: Cash Courses" (article available online from ReadWorks)

SAMPLE RESPONSE (FULL SCORE): WHY WOULD THIS RECEIVE A FULL SCORE?

The structure of "News Debate: Cash Courses" is compare/contrast. The article is set up like a debate with one section in favor of getting paid to do well in courses while the other section is against getting paid. One student argued that it's good for high school students to get paid for getting high grades because when they get money they try harder, and also they don't need an after-school job so they can study. But another student disagreed, saying that students should be able to motivate themselves. They should work hard because good grades will lead to better paying jobs in the future. I think the author chose this structure because with two points of view, you can compare the sections.

SAMPLE RESPONSE (PARTIAL SCORE): HOW COULD WE REVISE THIS FOR A FULL SCORE?

The structure of "News Debate: Cash Courses" is description. I know this because there are different main ideas. One main idea is that getting paid for grades is good. The other main idea is that getting paid for grades is bad. Students had lots of reasons like it won't cost the schools anything because people will donate money. I think the author chose a descriptive structure because there were two main ideas.

What kind of information does the author provide in [paragraph A] and why does the author include it?

Sample Question

In the article "The Tale of the Barnacle and the Whale" what kind of information does the author provide in the last paragraph (that begins "As you can see . . .") and why does the author include it?

Source: "The Tale of the Barnacle and the Whale" (article available online from ReadWorks)

SAMPLE RESPONSE (FULL SCORE): WHY WOULD THIS RECEIVE A FULL SCORE?

In the last paragraph of "The Tale of the Barnacle and the Whale," the author is comparing and contrasting whether the whale or the barnacles benefit most when barnacles live on a whale. First, the author says that barnacles benefit because they get food and protection. Then the author says, "The whales, on the other hand, don't benefit from this arrangement." A detail that proves this contrast is that having too many barnacles on them can make it harder for whales to swim through the water. But barnacles can also protect whales from predators. I think the author included this information to show what the relationship is like between barnacles and whales.

SAMPLE RESPONSE (PARTIAL SCORE): HOW COULD WE REVISE THIS FOR A FULL SCORE?

The last paragraph of "The Tale of the Barnacle and the Whale" explains that barnacles benefit a lot from living on whales because they get food and protection. Whales don't benefit as much. In fact, barnacles make it harder for them to swim. But barnacles might help whales fight other whales because the barnacles are sharp. I think the author wanted to show that barnacles are both good and bad.

How does [paragraph A] connect to [paragraph B]?

Sample Question

In "The Two Harriets," how does the paragraph that begins, "During the Civil War . . ." connect to the paragraph before it that begins, "Just one year after her own escape . . ."?

Source: "The Two Harriets, Heroines of Abolition" (article available online from ReadWorks)

SAMPLE RESPONSE (FULL SCORE): WHY WOULD THIS RECEIVE A FULL SCORE?

The paragraph in "The Two Harriets" that begins, "During the Civil War" is connected to the paragraph before it that begins "Just one year after her own escape" by changing the topic. The first paragraph talks about Harriet Tubman's work with the Underground Railroad. She returned to the South 19 times and she rescued 300 slaves. The next paragraph talks about what Harriet Tubman did when she was a spy. Once, she found out where the Confederate Army was hiding along the Combahee River. This was a good way to connect these paragraphs because the author wanted to show that Harriet helped her country in two ways, and why she was a hero.

SAMPLE RESPONSE (PARTIAL SCORE): HOW COULD WE REVISE THIS FOR A FULL SCORE?

The paragraph that begins, "During the Civil War" is connected to the paragraph that begins, "Just one year after her escape" by telling more about Harriet Tubman's life. She was a hero who helped slaves get to freedom on the Underground Railroad. She was also a spy for the Union Army. The author showed that Harriet Tubman really deserved to be called a hero.

Why did the author choose to begin/ end the story with this [paragraph]?

Sample Question

Why did the author, J.M. Barrie, choose to begin the story *Peter Pan* with the paragraph that starts: "All children, except one, grow up."?

Source: *Peter Pan* by J.M. Barrie (novel available online from Project Gutenburg)

SAMPLE RESPONSE (FULL SCORE): WHY WOULD THIS RECEIVE A FULL SCORE?

The author, J.M. Barrie, began *Peter Pan* with a mystery. He says, "All children, except one, grow up," which makes you want to know who didn't grow up and why they didn't grow up. It hooks you and keeps you reading. In this paragraph you also get introduced to two characters, Mrs. Darling and Wendy. You find out that Wendy is *not* the person who doesn't grow up because her mother (Mrs. Darling) says, "Oh, why can't you remain like this forever!" I think this is a good beginning to the story because you want to know more about Wendy and the mystery person who doesn't grow up. It also makes me curious about what happens to someone who doesn't grow up.

SAMPLE RESPONSE (PARTIAL SCORE): HOW COULD WE REVISE THIS FOR A FULL SCORE?

In the first paragraph of *Peter Pan*, you find out that Wendy brought her mother a flower from the garden one time when she was a little girl. Her mom, Mrs. Darling, thought she was cute and was sad she had to grow up. Even though she was only two years old, Wendy knew she had to grow up, too. I think this is a good beginning because you find out about Wendy and she is a character in the story.

Where is the flashback in this story and why did the author most likely include it?

Sample Question

Where is there a flashback in the story *Testing the Ice: A True Story about Jackie Robinson,* and what is the most likely reason the author included it?

Source: *Testing the Ice: A True Story about Jackie Robinson* by Sharon Robinson (picture book)

SAMPLE RESPONSE (FULL SCORE): WHY DOES THIS RESPONSE EARN A FULL SCORE?

There is a flashback in the middle of the story *Testing the Ice* when Jackie Robinson explains what it was like for a Black person to play professional baseball a long time ago. The pictures in this part of the book aren't in color like the rest of the story, which is how the author shows it is back in time. The flashback shows that Jackie had to overcome lots of challenges but these challenges made him stronger. One example was that at first, Black players couldn't play in the Major Leagues. Also, the teams went places where Black people weren't allowed in the same restaurants as white people. I think the flashback is important because it helps us understand more about racism.

SAMPLE RESPONSE (PARTIAL SCORE): HOW COULD WE REVISE THIS FOR A FULL SCORE?

Jackie Robinson was a great baseball player, but the flashback shows he couldn't always play in the Major Leagues. There was segregation back then and people called him names. The author wanted us to know about segregation.

What is the backstory for this [story], and why did the author most likely include it?

Sample Question

What is the backstory for "NASA Engineers Fix Glitch on Voyager 2 Spacecraft from 11.5 Billion Miles Away!" and why did the author most likely include it?

Source: "NASA Engineers Fix Glitch on Voyager 2 Spacecraft from 11.5 Billion Miles Away!" by Meera Dolasia (article available online)

SAMPLE RESPONSE (FULL SCORE):
WHY DOES THIS RESPONSE EARN A FULL SCORE?

This article is about scientists fixing a computer problem with Voyager 2 from billions of miles away. It took 17 hours to send information from Earth to the shuttle, and 17 more hours to find out if the command worked. But it did work!

At the end of the article, the author tells the backstory about Voyager 1 and 2. They were first launched in 1977 to do close-up studies of Jupiter and Saturn. They were so successful that they were later used to study more planets, their moons and the planets' magnetic fields. Now they are helping scientists learn more about the sun. I think the author included this backstory to help us better understand how the Voyager shuttles have made a big difference to our knowledge of space for many years.

SAMPLE RESPONSE (PARTIAL SCORE):
HOW COULD WE REVISE THIS FOR A FULL SCORE?

The article is about scientists fixing Voyager 2 so it could study the sun. It did get fixed, which is good. At the end of the article there's a backstory that tells about Voyager 1 and Voyager 2 when they first studied other planets and moons. It is important to understand the sun, planets, and moons, which is why the author included this information.

Why do you think the author included this quote from another author at the beginning of this [chapter]?

Sample Question

Why do you think the author included the quote from Ruby's mother at the beginning of the book, *The Story of Ruby Bridges*?

Source: *The Story of Ruby Bridges* by Robert Coles (picture book)

SAMPLE RESPONSE (FULL SCORE):
WHY DOES THIS RESPONSE EARN A FULL SCORE?

I think the author's main reason for including this quote from Ruby's mother about making a difference is to show the central idea of the story. The quote explains that even though she was a little girl, Ruby helped to change history. She did this by helping to end segregation in schools. When you read the story, you find out details that show what Ruby's mother means in this quote. For example, Ruby was brave and walked into a school that only white children had attended even though people screamed insults. Then when she was the only child in her class, this didn't keep Ruby away either. She stayed until the other children gave up protesting and came back. I think the author included this quote because it's important to see how Ruby made a difference in ending segregation.

SAMPLE RESPONSE (PARTIAL SCORE):
HOW COULD WE REVISE THIS FOR A FULL SCORE?

I think the author included this quote to show that Ruby taught us a lot of things like having Black people and white people get to know each other more. In the story, people were mean to Ruby, but she was never mean back to them. I think the author wanted us to know that Ruby's mother was proud of her.

How would this story change if it were told from [new narrator's] point of view?

Sample Question

How would the excerpt (first four paragraphs) from *The Velveteen Rabbit* change if it was written from the Rabbit's point of view?

Source: *The Velveteen Rabbit* by Margery Williams (children's book available online from Project Gutenburg)

SAMPLE RESPONSE (FULL SCORE): WHY DOES THIS RESPONSE EARN A FULL SCORE?

If *The Velveteen Rabbit* was written from the Rabbit's point of view, you could see this character's motivation, feelings, and attitude more clearly. You would see that the Rabbit just wants to be respected. That is his motivation. In the text it says, "Some of the more expensive toys quite snubbed him." You would see that his attitude was very humble, because the author says he is shy, and he thought he wasn't as good as the mechanical toys. He didn't want to mention that he was filled with sawdust because sawdust wasn't cool. Finally, for feelings, you would see that he was sad. The boy forgot about him when he got other presents. It would be good to tell this story from the Rabbit's point of view because you could see he is really hurting, like he needs a hug.

SAMPLE RESPONSE (PARTIAL SCORE): HOW COULD WE REVISE THIS FOR A FULL SCORE?

If *The Velveteen Rabbit* was written from the Rabbit's point of view, you would see he was motivated by wanting to fit in. The other toys didn't like him. His feelings were sad because the other toys didn't like him. He had a negative attitude, too. It's good to tell this story from the Rabbit's point of view because you can see he needs to have a better attitude and he needs to feel happy.

What is your point of view about _____, and how is it the same or different from the point of view of the author?

Sample Question

What is your point of view about zoos, and how is it the same or different from the point of view of the author?

Source: "Tiger Attack Spurs Debate" (article available online from ReadWorks)

SAMPLE RESPONSE (FULL SCORE): WHY WOULD THIS RECEIVE A FULL SCORE?

In the article "Tiger Attack Spurs Debate," I agree with the opinion that zoos are bad. It's not right to keep wild animals in captivity. Large animals like elephants and tigers need more space to roam around than they will get in a zoo, especially when they're kept in a cage. This leads to animals being unhappy. They pace back and forth or swim in circles. They are meant to hunt for food. But in a zoo, they have nothing to do but be bored. Another reason for not having zoos is that these big animals can be dangerous, especially when they can't handle captivity anymore. They might attack zoo workers or even visitors. Since 1990, at least four children and 15 adults have been killed. Some people argue that zoos are good because people get to see animals that they may not be able to see any other way. But that's no excuse for making wild animals live in captivity. We need to solve this problem because animals have rights, too!

SAMPLE RESPONSE (PARTIAL SCORE): HOW COULD WE REVISE THIS FOR A FULL SCORE?

I agree with the point of view that zoos should be banned. Wild animals can be dangerous. For example, a tiger got loose from one zoo. It attacked a zoo worker and then other workers had to shoot the tiger. Lots of people die every year because they get attacked by zoo animals. Some people like zoos because they like to see wild animals. But I disagree.

What was the author's purpose for including this [paragraph/sentence]?

Sample Question

What was the author's purpose for including paragraph #2 in "Taking Down the Green-Eyed Monster"?

Source: "Taking Down the Green-Eyed Monster" by Margie Markarian (article available online from ReadWorks)

SAMPLE RESPONSE (FULL SCORE): WHY WOULD THIS RECEIVE A FULL SCORE?

The purpose of this paragraph is to give lots of examples of what might make kids feel jealous. Some of the examples in this paragraph are: You might feel jealous if your friend starts hanging out with someone else instead of you. Maybe your best friend has a boyfriend and you don't. Sometimes kids feel jealous if they think their friend is smarter, a better athlete, a better artist, or has cooler clothes. I think the author includes these examples so everyone will connect with this article. It's normal to have jealous feelings, but there are things you can do to feel better.

SAMPLE RESPONSE (PARTIAL SCORE): HOW COULD WE REVISE THIS FOR A FULL SCORE?

This paragraph gives a lot of examples about why people get jealous. Maybe your friend is spending time with other friends now, not you. Or you think other people have more than you do, and that makes you mad. But someone will always have more than you. So, try not to feel jealous. It's bad for you.

How did this video add to your understanding of _____?

Sample Question

How did the video of "The Ballad of Birmingham" add to your understanding of the Birmingham church bombing?

Source: "The Ballad of Birmingham" by Dudley Randall (3:07) (video file available on YouTube)

Alternate Source: "Amazing Animals: Gorilla" (1:46) (video file available online from National Geographic Kids)

SAMPLE RESPONSE (FULL SCORE):
WHY WOULD THIS RECEIVE A FULL SCORE?

The video of the poem "The Ballad of Birmingham" told the same story as the poem about a little girl who wanted to march in a Freedom March to help end segregation in Alabama in 1963. Her mom wanted her to go to church instead where she would be safe. She obeyed, but she wasn't safe there. A bomb went off and killed four girls. The message about senseless harm to innocent children is the same as in the poem. Here, you also get to hear the poem sung with some of the lines repeated to show their importance. You see images like children being attacked by dogs and photographs of the four girls who were killed. These images made me understand the pain of these people much more, as well as the violence. I think this video was better than the poem because it showed even more emotions.

SAMPLE RESPONSE (PARTIAL SCORE):
HOW COULD WE REVISE THIS FOR A FULL SCORE?

The video of "The Ballad of Birmingham" told the same story as the poem. A little girl was killed by a bomb with some other children when she went to church. This video includes music that sounds sad and pictures of some of the lines. You see a girl with white gloves ready for church. You see a girl who had been beaten lying in the hospital. It was a sad, bad time and lots of children got hurt.

Why do you think the author included this illustration (or photograph)?

Sample Question

Why do you think the reporter included this photograph of the four girls from the Birmingham church bombing in the newspaper story about this event?

Source: Photograph of destruction from the bomb and pictures of the four young girls killed in the Birmingham church bombing, September 1963 (photograph available from internet search)

Alternate source: *Ivan: The Remarkable True Story of the Shopping Mall Gorilla* by Katherine Applegate (picture book)

SAMPLE RESPONSE (FULL SCORE): WHY WOULD THIS RECEIVE A FULL SCORE?

This photograph from the newspaper in 1963 shows the four girls killed in the Birmingham church bombing. It looks like the girls' school pictures. Also, the photo shows part of the church and the street where the bombing happened. There was a lot of destruction, even to cars. This photo made me feel sick because I could see even more than in the poem that these were regular kids like me and my friends and they died that day because of prejudice. I felt so bad for their parents. I think the reporter included this picture to show how innocent children lost their lives because of hate. It made me wonder: When will people finally stop being prejudiced about race?

SAMPLE RESPONSE (PARTIAL SCORE): HOW COULD WE REVISE THIS FOR A FULL SCORE?

The picture I'm writing about is the Birmingham church bombing with the four girls who got killed. You can also see the church in the picture and some people standing around. The poem didn't talk about that. The picture made me feel sad for the girls who lost their lives. I think the reporter wanted to show how horrible the killers were. My question is: Why did someone bomb the church?

Which details from [the text] are relevant to the argument that _____?

Sample Question

Which details from the article "SummerReads: Bikes & Boards—Catch a Wave" are relevant to the argument that surfing requires special conditions?

Source: "SummerReads: Bikes & Boards—Catch a Wave" (article available online from ReadWorks)

SAMPLE RESPONSE (FULL SCORE):
WHY WOULD THIS RECEIVE A FULL SCORE?

According to this article about surfing, people can't surf everywhere there are waves. The waves can't be too small. They have to be big and strong enough to support the surfer and the surfboard on top of it. A wave also must be long enough so the surfer can ride it for a while. These are reasons that it's hard to surf in lakes. There aren't enough of the right kind of waves. But oceans are usually good for surfing. Some oceans (like the oceans near California, Florida, and Hawaii) are better than others because they have the best slope to the ocean floor. It is important to know this information so you can have fun and surf safely.

SAMPLE RESPONSE (PARTIAL SCORE):
HOW COULD WE REVISE THIS FOR A FULL SCORE?

In the article about surfing it says that people have been riding on waves for 250 years. They used wooden boards to paddle out into the ocean. When the wave broke, some riders stood up to ride the wave back in. They did this in the ocean surf, so the activity was called surfing. Now people know more about where to surf and to choose the right waves. I once tried surfing and it was fun.

What additional evidence for _____ could the author have included to make the argument more convincing?

Sample Question

What additional evidence for finding the right place to surf could the author have included in this article to make the argument more convincing?

Source: "SummerReads: Bikes & Boards—Catch a Wave" (article available online from ReadWorks)

SAMPLE RESPONSE (FULL SCORE):
WHY WOULD THIS RECEIVE A FULL SCORE?

In this article about surfing, the author gives reasons that some places are better for surfing than others. Although these reasons were relevant, other kinds of evidence would have made the article more convincing. For example, maybe the author could have added some quotes from surfers about their favorite places to surf, and why they are so great. Also, the article could have used more facts. It said the slope of the ocean floor was important for good surfing, but it never said what the slope should be. Finally, maybe there could have been a story from someone who had chosen a bad place to surf and what happened because of this bad choice. Adding more evidence would have made this article more convincing and would have helped people make good choices about where to surf.

SAMPLE RESPONSE (PARTIAL SCORE):
HOW COULD WE REVISE THIS FOR A FULL SCORE?

This author gives a lot of good information about where to surf. But if other evidence were added, it would make the article more convincing. For example, there could be some statistics because numbers make things believable. Maybe there could be some quotes from experts, too. If it was a famous surfer who was quoted, that would be convincing.

Which source does a better job of explaining _____? Cite specific evidence to support your answer.

Sample Question

Which source, "The Continental Army at Valley Forge" or "The Revolutionary War: Valley Forge," does a better job of explaining why the Continental Army was in such bad shape when soldiers arrived in Valley Forge in the winter of 1777–1778? Cite specific evidence to support your answer.

Sources

"The Continental Army at Valley Forge, 1777" (web page available at EyeWitnesstoHistory.com)

"The Revolutionary War: Valley Forge" (article available online from ReadWorks)

SAMPLE RESPONSE (FULL SCORE):
WHY WOULD THIS RECEIVE A FULL SCORE?

The article "The Continental Army at Valley Forge" does a better job of explaining why the Continental Army was in terrible shape when it arrived at Valley Forge because it gives more details. It explains that first the British army fought the Americans in Brandywine, near Philadelphia in September and defeated them. Then the Americans lost another battle to the British in Germantown in October. Also, they tried to move the capital, which was tiring. They were "weary and demoralized." The "Valley Forge" article only says that the Americans lost twice to the British.

SAMPLE RESPONSE (PARTIAL SCORE):
HOW COULD WE REVISE THIS FOR A FULL SCORE?

"The Continental Army at Valley Forge" did a better job of explaining why the American soldiers were in bad shape when they got to Valley Forge for the winter. Both articles say that there were two battles in the fall and the British won them both. But the first article gives more details about the battles. You can picture the soldiers being very tired. At the camp, conditions were terrible. Lots of soldiers died.

Explain how each of the selections you read about [topic] could be useful to someone writing about this topic.

Sample Question

Explain how each of the articles you read ("The Two Harriets, Heroines of Abolition" and "Slavery, Civil War & Reconstruction—The Underground Railroad") could be useful to someone writing about ending slavery.

Sources:

"Slavery, Civil War & Reconstruction—The Underground Railroad" (article available online from ReadWorks)

"The Two Harriets, Heroines of Abolition" (article available online from ReadWorks)

SAMPLE RESPONSE (FULL SCORE):
WHY WOULD THIS RECEIVE A FULL SCORE?

Both of these articles could be useful for writing about ending slavery. The "Underground Railroad" article <u>defined</u> the words *Underground Railroad, stations,* and *conductors.* "The Two Harriets" defined *abolitionists.* I would include all these words. There were lots of <u>facts</u> in both articles that would go into my report. "The Underground Railroad" had facts about how to help slaves escape. Most of the facts in "The Two Harriets" told about Harriet Tubman and how she made many trips to the South to get slaves. The best <u>story</u> from the articles was in "The Two Harriets." It was about Harriet Beecher Stowe and how she wrote *Uncle Tom's Cabin.*

SAMPLE RESPONSE (PARTIAL SCORE):
HOW COULD WE REVISE THIS FOR A FULL SCORE?

There is lots of information in these articles about ending slavery. In the article "The Underground Railroad" there were <u>definitions</u> like *Underground Railroad, conductors,* and *stations.* There were <u>facts</u> about the Underground Railroad. "The Two Harriets" had a <u>definition</u> for *abolitionist* and lots of <u>facts</u> about Harriet Tubman and how she helped slaves run away. In this article there is also a <u>story</u> about mean treatment of slaves by their masters.

Use the information from these [two] sources to write a diary entry from your point of view, imagining that you are personally experiencing the situation identified in these sources. Be sure to include details from the informational sources you read.

Sample Question

Use the information from "The Oregon Trail: Fun Facts" and "Westward Expansion—The Oregon Trail" to write a diary entry from your point of view, imagining that you are heading west in a covered wagon with your family. Be sure to include details from the informational sources you read.

Sources

"The Oregon Trail" (web page available at AmericanHistoryforKids.com)

"Westward Expansion—The Oregon Trail" (article available online from ReadWorks)

SAMPLE RESPONSE (FULL SCORE):
WHY WOULD THIS RECEIVE A FULL SCORE?

1845, Sometime in the Spring

Dear Diary,

It has been many weeks since we set out from Missouri in this wagon train. My dad is excited to go to Oregon because the land there is supposed to be great for farming but traveling in our covered wagon is awful. There isn't enough room for me to ride inside, so I have to walk the whole way. I don't have any shoes, so my feet are killing me. The trail is all rutted and full of sharp twigs and little stones. Today I saw a huge snake! At least everyone in my family is still healthy. My mom's friend got sick from something called cholera and died. Maybe she just starved to death because we don't have much food. I hope my dad is right that getting to Oregon is worth all this misery. One thing I do like is the campfires at night. We all sit in a circle and sing songs. That keeps my spirits up and my feet get a rest.

Your friend, Nancy

SAMPLE RESPONSE (PARTIAL SCORE):
HOW COULD WE REVISE THIS FOR A FULL SCORE?

1845, sometime in the Spring

Dear Diary,

We are traveling to Oregon in a covered wagon. The trail is very pretty with nice flowers and I picked some today. I gave them to my mom and she liked them. I can't wait to get to Oregon, and I hope I make friends there. I hope my dad gets a big farm. Maybe we will even get rich. That would be nice. I wonder if they have schools in Oregon. I want to go to a real school.

Identify the central idea in Source #1 and Source #2. Then compare and contrast the way the author develops the central idea in each of the sources.

Sample Question

Identify the central idea in "The Lion and the Mouse" and "The Ant and the Dove." Then compare and contrast the way the author develops the central idea in each of the sources.

Sources

"The Lion and the Mouse" by Aesop (fable available online from Project Gutenburg)

"The Ant and the Dove" by Aesop (fable available online from Project Gutenburg)

SAMPLE RESPONSE (FULL SCORE): WHY DOES THIS RESPONSE EARN A FULL SCORE?

Paragraph 1

In Source #1, "The Lion and the Mouse" and in Source #2 "The Ant and the Dove" the central idea is: If you do something kind for someone, they may do something kind for you in return. In both sources, something bad happened to the first character, and the second character helped. Then the first character helped the second character when he was in trouble. One big difference was that the Lion was very mean at the beginning. The Dove was kind.

Paragraph 2: What happens in Source #1 that shows the central idea?

Here is what happens in Source #1, "The Lion and the Mouse." A little Mouse was crawling up a Lion's tail when the lion woke up and said he would eat him. But the Mouse begged to be let go and the lion let him go, even though the Lion wasn't nice to him. He said, "How could you help me? You're just a little Mouse." Later the Lion got caught in a trap and the little Mouse chewed through the rope so the Lion wouldn't die. The Lion was wrong. The Mouse could help him.

Paragraph 3: What happens in Source #2 that shows the central idea?

Here is what happens in Source #2, "The Ant and the Dove." First, an Ant fell into a brook and couldn't swim to shore. He would have drowned but the Dove gave him a leaf to float on. Then a man was going to kill the Dove by setting a trap, but the Ant stung him so the man was in pain and ran away before he could capture the Dove.

Final Paragraph: Explain why this central idea is important

I will remember these stories and try to do something nice for my brother like let him ride my new bike. Then maybe he will let me try his new iPad. I'll try to be like the Dove, not the Lion because the Dove was kind about helping and at first the Lion was mean. If you're trying to be helpful, you shouldn't be mean about it.

SAMPLE RESPONSE (PARTIAL SCORE): HOW COULD WE REVISE THIS FOR A FULL SCORE?

The central idea in "The Lion and the Mouse" and "The Ant and the Dove" is the same. It is that you should be nice to other people. At first the Lion was not nice to the Mouse. He wanted to eat him, but he didn't. Later the Mouse was nice to the Mouse when he helped him get free. The Ant and the Dove were always nice to each other.

ANALYSIS OF SAMPLE PARTIAL SCORE RESPONSES

Responses that received a partial score were designed to show the kinds of errors students typically make when answering constructed response questions. The most common shortcoming is that students offer evidence that is general rather than specific—although the text provided ample details. Other frequent deficiencies include inaccuracies, perhaps the result of reading too quickly, and disorganization where an answer repeats an idea over and over. When you analyze these responses with your students, be sure to talk with them about how they can avoid similar problems with their own responses.

Question 1.1: Which details are most surprising?
This student identifies the surprise correctly, but offers only one piece of evidence despite the many details provided in the text. The student also misses the key point: making assumptions such as this are based on stereotypes. In fact, this student shows gender bias when she says this is unacceptable "girl" behavior. (But what is she saying about "boy" behavior?)

Question 1.2: Which details were the most helpful in figuring out _____?
This student reaches the right conclusion, but the details provided are not convincing. For example, wearing leather clothes and not talking don't lead logically to anything related to cold weather.

Question 2.1: Paraphrase this [paragraph] to show its meaning in your own words.
This response is more of a summary than a paraphrasing. It misses some of the key information like the mention of friends and where the child goes at night (The Land of Nod).

Question 2.2: How does the author develop the idea of _____?
There are too few details here to see the *development* of the central idea (hope). The ending repeats an earlier claim without explaining the importance.

Question 2.3: What is the central idea/theme of _____ and how does the author develop it?
The biggest problem with this response is that the student misses the central idea. It is true that the Bees made the honey, not the Wasps, but that's not the message. The

central idea here (or moral) is that it's one thing to *say* you have a skill, but then you should be able to demonstrate it.

Question 2.4: What is the main idea of this [paragraph] and how does the author develop it?

This student missed the point that this question asked for the main idea, and instead just gives her opinion. She does use evidence from the text, but in defense of her own view.

Question 2.5: Briefly summarize this story including only the key points.

This is a fair start and does include several key points: characters' name, where the story takes place, the importance of the cat, and something about the ending. But there is no mention of the importance (how Spaghetti changed Gabriel's life) and additional details from the middle of the story like those the first model included.

Question 2.6: What conclusion can you draw about [character, problem, etc.]?

This response focuses only on what Molly Pitcher *did*, not what her actions meant or the importance of her actions. It misses the key point that Molly was a *woman*, and no one expected such bravery from a female. This response also indicates that the Yankees won. It does not say this in the poem, and in fact, this battle is considered a draw. Above all, a response must be *accurate*. Always check for accuracy when scoring a response.

Question 3.1: What character trait (or feeling) does [character] mainly show in this story?

The character trait is accurate. There is some repetitive thinking here, and no details or explanation of importance.

Question 3.2: What is the character's attitude, and how does it make a difference?

This student chose a different attitude, but it works, so that is fine. The response includes one example that shows this attitude. It also identifies the lesson. But there is no mention of how the boy's attitude makes a difference, what might have caused it, or how it matters to the story.

Question 3.3: What motivated [character] to _____?

The motivation is not correct (the daughter's safety). There are no specific details to support the claim. There is no explanation of importance.

Question 3.4: What is the relationship between [Character A] and [Character B]?

The statement about the relationship is fine, but the student doesn't provide enough details about what happened in the story. It's hard to see how the details connect to the problem. There is at least brief mention of the importance.

Question 3.5: What is [Character's/Author's] point of view about _____? How does the character (or author) show this?

This student is correct about the point of view, but there are no specific details about the good things that happened to him. There is also no explanation of importance.

Question 3.6: What are the most important differences between [Character A] and [Character B]?

This student identified a key difference—Fern's and Mr. Arable's different feelings about the pig. However, the details about Fern are very general, and the student missed the *reason* for Mr. Arable's feelings: the pig was getting expensive to feed. There is also no mention of the solution to the problem, that made both Fern and her dad happy—that Fern could still visit Wilbur.

Question 3.7: What is the relationship between [the setting] and [the problem] in _____?

This student veers off-track with a focus on football. Although the response references the problems that Indians faced at Indian schools, it doesn't seem clear about how the problem and the setting are connected.

Question 4.1: What does [word] mean and what clue in the text helped you to understand it?

This was an honest mistake. The student did look for a clue but overlooked the better one and instead focused on an example that was incorrect. The right clue might have been easier to spot if the conjunction in the line was *but*: "This one is sailing *but* that one is moored." Authors don't always "play by the rules."

Question 4.2: What word might the author use to make the meaning in this [sentence] clearer?

Hiked is a more precise word and does provide a better mental image. However, it doesn't convey the tone. The student should have chosen a word that is logical for the whole paragraph—which would be different in this case for Paragraph 1 and Paragraph 2.

Question 4.3: What words create the tone in this [paragraph]? What is the tone?

This student has determined a tone that is acceptable. However, there is only one detail from the text provided as evidence. It is always best to identify a tone that has substantial evidence. If the student can't find additional defense, it would be good to choose a different tone word that had more support in the text.

Question 4.4: What author's craft (like description, dialogue, internal dialogue, and gesture) does the author use in this [part of the story] and why do you think the author included it?

This is actually quite a good answer and doesn't need much improvement. It is included to show what an answer focused on *gesture* might look like. The one omission here was a concluding statement to pull together what you learn about Peter's overall character from these small actions.

Question 4.5: What figurative language (like simile, metaphor, personification, idiom, or hyperbole) does the author use in this [paragraph] and why do you think the author chose it?

This student correctly identified the figurative language (personification). But the response is more of a summary than a clarification of where to find examples of personification. Specific textual evidence is needed here. Also, there is no mention of how this figurative language makes the writing stronger.

Question 4.6: What elements of a [fable] did you find in this text? Find at least two elements and explain how the author uses them.

This student named two fable elements accurately, but didn't provide much textual evidence, and in fact, missed the moral. More than a *writing* problem, this is a *comprehension* problem, and should be addressed before revising the answer.

Question 4.7: Why do you think the author wrote this as a [poem]?

A quality answer to a question about poetry will include lots of specifics about language—which this response lacks. The answer is very general with no details about *how* the author uses language (imagery, figurative language, etc.). Quotes from the text would also be helpful.

Question 5.1: What is this text feature and what is the most likely reason the author included it?

This student names the text feature accurately but isn't specific enough about what the graph shows. Also, there's some repetitive thinking. The student mentions over and over that China has a bigger population, but is not insightful about why the author would want to show this.

Question 5.2: What text structure did the author choose for writing [about this topic] and what is the most likely reason the author chose it?

This student is correct that there are two main ideas, but missed the point that a *better* answer is that the author is comparing and contrasting those ideas. Also, the response would have been stronger if the student had provided a detail from each argument to show the contrast.

Question 5.3: What kind of information does the author provide in [paragraph A] and why does the author include it?

This student seems to have understood the content of this paragraph but doesn't recognize that the question asks about the *structure*, not just the content. Although the student may understand this, there is no mention of the paragraph's purpose, which is to compare and contrast. This is why this response couldn't receive a full score.

Question 5.4: How does [paragraph A] connect to [paragraph B]?

This student understood why Harriet Tubman was considered a hero, and the student is also correct that Harriet was helpful in two different ways. However, there is no mention of the specific ways that the two paragraphs are connected. The student should also provide evidence from the text that shows Harriet's work on the Underground Railroad and as a spy.

Question 5.5: Why did the author choose to begin/ end the story with this [paragraph]?

The main problem with this response is that the student doesn't identify the craft the author uses to begin the story. There is mention at the end about learning about a character (Wendy), but a key point here is the mystery in the first short sentence (that one child didn't grow up). The author wants readers to recognize this as it is critical to the development of the plot.

Question 5.6: Where is the flashback in the story and why did the author most likely include it?

Although this response isn't well organized, the student has some of the essential information, including the content of the flashback and what it showed. More is needed regarding the reason for the flashback: the kind of discrimination that Jackie experienced.

Question 5.7: What is the backstory for this [story], and why did the author most likely include it?

This student seems to have an adequate understanding of this article but doesn't include enough specific details. The response misses the key point that scientists were able to fix the problem from billions of miles away. The student also needed to be more thoughtful about *why* it is important to understand the sun, planets, and moons.

Question 5.8: Why do you think the author included this quote from another author at the beginning of this [chapter]?

One of the problems with this response is that the student mostly reorganizes the words in the quote without providing much interpretation. There are also no textual details to show how people were mean to Ruby, or how she responded. The writer does not specify the purpose of the quote (to mirror the central idea), and the explanation of importance at the end, while accurate, could be more insightful—Ruby's role in helping to end segregation.

Question 6.1: How would this story change if it were told from [new narrator's] point of view?

"Fitting in" is a valid motivation, so that part of the response is fine. However, there's no specific evidence provided to show that the other toys didn't like him. And then the student repeats the same general detail for feelings. The attitude could have been more specific than just "negative." The explanation at the end, while devoid of compassion (and not what we'd hope a student would think), is an opinion, and hence acceptable from a scoring perspective.

Question 6.2: What is your point of view about _____, and how is it the same or different from the point of view of the author?

This answer is generally correct, but there was lots of specific evidence in this article that the student chose not to include. A strong argument will include *all* of the best evidence. There is also no explanation of importance.

Question 6.3: What was the author's purpose for including this [paragraph/sentence]?

Although the student correctly identifies the reason for the paragraph as providing examples and supplies appropriate supporting details, *why* the author included this information is inaccurate. The end of the paragraph transitions to the idea that there are strategies for dealing with jealousy.

Question 7.1: How did this video add to your understanding of _____?

This response starts strong by telling the story of what happens in the video, and then explains the message. It also identifies some of the powerful images. But then the student goes offtrack, repeating the message over and over—without describing how the video added to the meaning of the poem itself.

Question 7.2: Why do you think the author included this illustration (or photograph)?

The beginning of this response is adequate but doesn't go into much detail about the feelings generated by the picture. The statement of the author's purpose is superficial as well. The lingering question about why the church was bombed would have been answered in the companion poem "The Ballad of Birmingham" before students viewed this photograph.

Question 8.1: Which details from [the text] are relevant to the argument that _____?

This student basically summarized the whole article, forgetting to focus on exactly what the question asked. Some details are not relevant to the question. Also, the student did not end with a statement about importance, which would be critical in this case.

Question 8.2: What additional evidence for _____ could the author have included to make the argument more convincing?

This student has good ideas about additional evidence but doesn't explain enough about what the evidence would show. Statistics about what? What questions would you want an expert to answer? The student does provide a good wrap-up sentence.

Question 9.1: Which source does a better job of explaining _____? Cite specific evidence to support your answer.

This answer begins well, accurately noting the strength of the first article. The student mentions that the first article told more about the battles but doesn't provide any evidence. Also, the question does not ask about camp conditions, so the final couple of sentences should not have been included in this response.

Question 9.2: Explain how each of the selections you read about [topic] could be useful to someone writing about this topic.

Although this student gives most of the same details from both articles, the information is not *integrated*. When you write a report, you don't write all the information from the first article, then move on to the information from the second article. You put the information *together*: the important words from each article, then the facts, and so on.

Question 9.3: Use the information from these [two] sources to write a diary entry from your point of view, imagining that you are personally experiencing the situation identified in these sources. Be sure to include details from the informational sources you read.
This is a nice little story and shows lots of the narrator's feelings. But there are very few details from either source that are included.

Question 9.4: Identify the central idea in Source #1 and Source #2. Then compare and contrast the way the author develops the central idea in each of the sources.
This response is too general. Even the initial inference is not specific enough. Students need to recognize that if you are kind (nice) to someone, they may be nice to you in return. There are not enough story details about either story, especially for "The Ant and the Dove." Also, there is no mention of the importance of the message and how the reader can relate to it beyond the texts themselves.

CHAPTER 8

ANSWER FRAMES FOR CONSTRUCTED RESPONSE

Once upon a time, in a land before Common Core, when states all had their own standards and their own standards-based assessments, my work took me into lots of classrooms. I saw how students struggled with constructed response, which was heavily tested on "the big test," and how frustrated teachers became when trying to offer help. I wanted to help too, so I wrote a book called *That's a Great Answer*. At that time, I was focused exclusively on supporting the writing, not the underlying reading or language issues that impacted constructed response. The book was a compilation of answer frames. *Lots* of answer frames. They were poised to achieve what answer frames are designed to do—lead students to success.

Answer frames support writers in several ways. First, they provide a logical structure. Many students have good thoughts dancing around in their brain, but don't know where to begin to get them on paper in an order that makes sense. Sometimes their written answers go around and around with information repeated and a sequence that doesn't seem sequential at all, regardless of how hard you work to sort it out as you read and reread it.

Another way frames support readers is that they clarify the kind of evidence to include, and how much evidence is needed, because the sentence stems prompt them: *One detail from the text that shows this character trait is _____. Another detail that shows this character trait is _____.* Moreover, the blank lines following the prompt alert the student to the approximate amount of space they'll probably need to answer that part of the question.

A final point in favor of frames is that they show what responses will look like as connected text, with sentences flowing from one to the next forming a paragraph. Alternately, some frames are written so that each new part of the response begins on a new line. I don't like this format as well because it sends the message that a constructed response is a series of discrete short answers.

Teachers loved *That's a Great Answer,* perhaps a little too much, seeing in the book's collection of answer frames a quick solution to a long-standing problem. That first book is now out of print, because life has moved on: there are new standards, new standards-based assessments with questions that require more rigor from students, and most importantly, new insights that answer frames alone will not get the job done.

Answer frames have always been the "sparkly thing," the scaffold that gets everyone's attention because they almost guarantee student success—in the short term. Powerful though answer frames can be, they are only effective when they take their rightful place among other supports, toward the end of an instructional sequence.

In the virtual lesson, you saw that I pulled out the answer frame as our session was winding down. You saw that even third-graders were willing to dive in and complete the response, and that they wrote quality answers. They could do this because they had a foundation upon which to build: an understanding of central idea based on a brief minilesson, an anchor chart to practice finding the central idea in today's texts, and the opportunity to rehearse their response before writing it using a cue card.

In future lessons, you'd not only want to review the steps to writing a good answer, you'd want to gradually remove the answer frame until students no longer need it. Move systematically toward this goal. If you don't, those prized answer frames lead to dependence and learned helplessness rather than self-sufficiency.

And a final note: Answer frames will not be "prized" by everyone in your class. They will be a blessing to students who need the graphic support (or perhaps even the emotional support) to write a response. But for students who don't need an organizer, these frames will feel constraining. Please do not make it mandatory for students to use answer frames if they do fine without them.

The answer frames that follow are organized in the same order as the comprehension questions beginning with Standard 1 and ending with Standard 9. Note that the answer frames can be photocopied from the book or downloaded and printed from https://wwnorton.com/AwesomeAnswers, for distribution to students.

Which details are most surprising?

Name: _____ Date: _____

Steps to a great answer

1. Choose an <u>important</u> detail in the text that is very surprising.

2. Explain *why* this detail is surprising: Why didn't you expect this to happen?

3. Find at least two pieces of evidence that show why you were surprised.

4. Explain why this surprise is important: What does it show about the character or the situation?*

*If there are other important surprises, write about them following steps 1–4.

In _____, it was very sur-
TITLE OF SOURCE
prising when _____

_____.

This was surprising because _____

_____

_____.

Some evidence that shows this is: _____

_____

_____.

This surprise was important because_____

_____.

Which details were the most helpful in figuring out _____?

Name: _____ **Date:** _____

Steps to a great answer

1. Identify the detail that was the most helpful in solving the mystery.

2. State what you figured out.

3. Explain *why* this clue was the most helpful.

4. Tell other clues that fit with the best clue, and *why*.

5. (Optional) Tell other clues that were *not* as helpful and why they weren't helpful.

In _____, the most helpful
 TITLE
detail in figuring out the mystery of _____

_____ was _____

_____.

This helped me figure out that _____

_____

_____.

Other details that fit with this clue were _____

_____.

Some details that were not very helpful were: _____

_____

_____. They weren't helpful because _____

_____.

Paraphrase this [paragraph] to show its meaning in your own words.

Name: _____ Date: _____

Steps to a great answer

1. Read the passage a few times to make sure you understand it.

2. Decide the words you need to keep (like names of places, people's names, and dates).

3. Decide which words can be changed and find synonyms that mean about the same thing. (You might want to use a thesaurus for this.)

4. Decide how you will rearrange some sentences or combine sentences.

5. Decide how you start your [paragraph], making sure it's different from the author's version.

6. Write *your* [paragraph] without looking at the author's [paragraph].

Because all paraphrased passages will be different, no sentence starters are provided for this response.

_____

_____

_____

_____

_____

_____

How does the author develop the idea of _____?

Name: _____ **Date:** _____

Steps to a great answer

1. Write a sentence that states the claim (what you're proving).

2. Choose a detail from the text that shows the situation at the beginning of the text.

3. Choose a detail from the text that shows how the situation develops.

4. Choose a detail from the text that shows how the situation ends.*

5. Explain what the situation <u>shows</u>; its importance.

*Note that you can include more details if you want. Consider including a quote for added support.

In _____,
                                    TITLE OF TEXT
the author develops the idea of _____
_____.

In the beginning, _____

_____

_____

_____

_____

_____

_____.

Then, _____

_____

_____

_____

_____

_____.

Finally, _____

_____

_____

_____

_____

_____.

This situation showed that _____

_____

_____

_____

_____

_____

_____.

What is the central idea/theme of _____ and how does the author develop it?

Name: _____   **Date:** _____

Steps to a great answer

1. Figure out the central idea and state it in your first sentence.

2. Choose a detail from the text that shows the situation at the beginning of the text.

3. Choose a detail from the text that shows how the situation develops.

4. Choose a detail from the text that shows how the situation ends.*

* Note that you can include more details if you want. Consider including a quote for added support.

In _____,
TITLE OF TEXT
the author develops the idea of _____
_____.

In the beginning, _____
_____
_____
_____
_____
_____
_____.

Then, _____
_____
_____
_____
_____
_____.

Finally, _____
_____
_____
_____
_____
_____.

This shows something important about this central idea: _____
_____
_____
_____
_____
_____.

What is the main idea of this [paragraph] and how does the author develop it?

Name: _____ Date: _____

Steps to a great answer

1. Find a sentence in the [passage] that states the main idea or infer it and write a first sentence that states this main idea.

2. Choose one piece of evidence that supports the main idea and write a sentence or two about it. (You can include a quote for additional support.)

3. Choose a second piece of evidence that supports the main idea and write a sentence or two about it. (You can include a quote for additional support.)

4. If there's more evidence you'd like to include, write about this evidence, too.

Explain the importance of the issue, possibly by describing why it matters, and to whom.

In _____,

                                      TITLE OF PASSAGE OR TEXT

the main idea is_____

_____

_____

_____.

The author says, _____

_____

_____

_____

_____.

The author also says, _____

_____

_____

_____

_____.

This issue is important because _____

_____

_____

_____

_____.

Briefly summarize this story including only the key points.

Name: _____ Date: _____

Steps to a great answer

1. Explain what happens at the <u>beginning</u> of the story, including the main characters, where the action takes place, and the problem.

2. Explain what happens in the <u>middle</u> of the story, including road-blocks to solving the problem or steps to finding a solution.

3. Explain what happens at the <u>end</u> of the story, including how the problem gets solved and how the story ends.

4. Explain the importance, which may be the central idea and the lesson that was learned by the characters, or by you. (You could begin with this central idea rather than ending with it if you prefer.)

In _____, _____ was
        TITLE OF STORY   NAME OF MAIN CHARACTER

_____.
            WHERE WAS THE CHARACTER

The problem was _____

_____

_____.

The problem didn't get solved right away. Here's what happened on

the way to solving the problem: _____

_____

_____

_____.

At the end of the story, the problem got solved when _____

_____

_____

_____.

This story taught something important about _____

_____

_____

_____.

What conclusion can you draw about [character, problem, etc.]?

Name: _____ Date: _____

Steps to a great answer

1. State your conclusion including the title of the text that you read.

2. Write about one detail that supports your conclusion, possibly including a quote for extra proof.

3. Write about another detail to support your conclusion, possibly including a quote for extra proof. (You can include other details if you can find them.)

4. Explain why your conclusion is meaningful.

One conclusion I can draw about _____
WHAT ARE YOU DRAWING A CONCLUSION ABOUT?

in _____ is _____
NAME OF SOURCE

_____

_____

_____ .

A detail that shows this is _____

_____

_____

_____

_____ .

Another detail that shows this is _____
_____
_____
_____
_____
_____.

This is an important inference because _____
_____
_____
_____
_____
_____.

What character trait (or feeling) does [character] mainly show in this story?

Name: _____ **Date:** _____

Steps to a great answer

1. Decide what the <u>main</u> character trait (or feeling) is in the story (or in this part of the story).

2. Give one detail from the story that shows this trait (or feeling), including a quote if possible.

3. Give another detail from the story that shows this trait (or feeling)—if you can find a second detail. Again, include a quote for extra support.

4. Explain why this trait (or feeling) is important.

In this story (or in this part of the story), the character trait (feeling)

_____ <u>mainly</u> shows is _____.
<small>CHARACTER</small>

One detail in the story that shows this is when _____

_____

_____ .

Here is a quote that shows this: "_____

_____

_____

_____ ."

Another detail that shows this is when _____

_____

_____

_____.

This trait (feeling) is important to _____ because
CHARACTER

_____

_____

_____.

What is the character's attitude, and how does it make a difference?

Name: _____ Date: _____

Steps to a great answer

1. Identify the character and the attitude.
2. Give one example from the text with evidence of this attitude.
3. Give another example from the text that shows this attitude.
4. Explain why the character might have this attitude.
5. Explain how this character's attitude is important to the story.

In this story _____'s attitude was _____
                        CHARACTER'S NAME
_____.

An example from the text that shows this is _____

_____

_____

_____.

Another example that shows this is _____

_____

_____

_____.

The reason for this attitude may have been _____

_____

_____

_____.

This character's attitude made a difference to the story because ____

_____

_____

_____.

What motivated [character] to _____?

Name: _____ **Date:** _____

Steps to a great answer

1. Decide what motivated this character or person to take action.

2. Explain what problem the character or person was motivated to solve. Include at least one detail from the text.

3. Explain what happened as a result of the character's action to solve his problem? Include at least two details from the text. (Try to include a quote.)

4. Explain what this shows about this character or person at this point in the story.

5. Tell whether the character's motivation changed later in the story. Explain using details.

6. Explain what you learned from this story about motivation.

In _____,
TITLE OF STORY

_____ was motivated by
NAME OF CHARACTER OR PERSON

_____.

He/she wanted to _____

_____

_____.

Here is what the character did: _____

_____

_____

_____

_____

_____

_____

_____.

This shows something important about this character: _____

_____

_____

_____.

At the end of the story, the character's motivation [changed/didn't change]. I know this because _____

_____

_____

_____.

This story taught me something important about motivation: _____

_____

_____

_____.

What is the relationship between [Character A] and [Character B]?

Name: _____ Date: _____

Steps to a great answer

1. Decide whether the relationship was positive or negative and choose a specific word that describes this positive or negative relationship.

2. Choose one detail from the text that shows this relationship. Consider including a quote for extra support.

3. Choose a second detail from the text that shows this relationship. Consider including a quote for extra support.

4. Explain the importance of what was learned in this story about relationships.

In _____,
TITLE OF STORY

_____ and
NAME OF CHARACTER A

_____
NAME OF CHARACTER B

had a relationship that was _____.
POSITIVE / NEGATIVE

I would describe this relationship as _____

_____.
CHOOSE A SPECIFIC WORD FROM THE CHART: *ANALYZING CHARACTER RELATIONSHIPS*

One detail from the story that shows this is _____

_____

_____

_____

_____.

Another detail from the story that shows this is _____

_____

_____

_____

_____

_____.

The important thing about relationships to understand from this

story is _____

_____

_____

_____

_____.

What is [Character's/Author's] point of view about _____? How does the character (or author) show this?

Name: _____ **Date:** _____

Steps to a great answer

1. Decide what the character or author believes about the issue: Are they for it or against it? State this in your first sentence.

2. Choose one piece of evidence from the text that shows this point of view. (Think about why this is *good* evidence.) Consider including a quote for extra support.

3. Choose a second piece of evidence from the text that shows this point of view. (Think about why this is *good* evidence.) Consider including a quote for extra support.

4. Explain why this point of view is important to the character, the author, or to you.

In _____,
TITLE OF SOURCE
character's/author's point of view about _____

was _____

_____.

One detail that shows this is _____

_____

_____

_____.

Another detail that shows this is _____

_____

_____

_____.

The important thing to remember about this point of view is _____

_____

_____.

What are the most important differences between [Character A] and [Character B]?

Name: _____   **Date:** _____

Steps to a great answer

1. State one important difference between Character A and Character B.

2. Choose a detail from the text that shows this difference. Consider including a quote for extra support.

3. State another important difference between Character A and Character B.

4. Choose a detail from the text that shows this difference. Consider including a quote for extra support.

5. Explain why the difference between the characters is important.

In _____,
TITLE OF SOURCE
one important difference between _____
CHARACTER A
and _____ is _____
CHARACTER B
_____
_____.

One detail that shows this is _____
_____
_____
_____.

Another important difference is _____

_____

_____

_____ .

A detail that shows this is _____

_____

_____

_____ .

These differences are important because _____

_____

_____

_____ .

What is the relationship between [the setting] and [the problem] in _____?

Name: _____ **Date:** _____

Steps to a great answer

1. Identify the setting of the story or event.

2. Identify the problem in the story or event and show evidence of this problem with two or more details.

3. Explain how the setting mattered to the problem and how the situation might be different today.

4. Explain why it is important to understand *when* and *where* this situation took place.

In _____, the setting was
  TITLE OF STORY

_____
  WHERE AND WHEN DID THIS TAKE PLACE?

_____.

The problem was _____

_____

_____.

Two examples that showed this problem were _____

_____

_____

_____

_____

_____

_____.

This situation would be different today because _____

_____

_____

_____.

It is important to understand when and where this situation took

place because _____

_____

_____

_____.

What does [word] mean and what clue in the text helped you to understand it?

Name: _____ **Date:** _____

Steps to a great answer

1. Name the text you are reading and tell what the word means.

2. Identify the clue in the text that helped you understand the meaning.

3. Explain *how* this clue helped.

In_____,
TITLE OF TEXT

_____ means
THE IDENTIFIED WORD

_____

_____

The clue in the text that helped me understand this is _____

_____

_____

_____.

This was helpful because _____

_____

_____

_____.

What word might the author use to make the meaning in this [sentence] clearer?

Name: _____ Date: _____

Steps to a great answer

1. State the "old" word and the new word that is more precise.

2. Explain why you think the new word makes the meaning clearer.

In this [sentence] I would change the word _____
OLD WORD

to _____.
NEW WORD

I think this is a more precise word because _____

_____

_____

_____.

What words create the tone in this [paragraph]? What is the tone?

Name: _____ Date: _____

Steps to a great answer

1. Explain what the author uses tone words to describe. (This will probably be characters/people, place/setting, or events.)

2. Identify at least two words that show this tone. (More might be better.)

3. Name the tone that these words show and explain *why*.

4. If there are other words in the passage that show a different tone, repeat steps 1–3 and explain how the two tones work together.

In this [paragraph] the author chooses tone words to describe

_____.
CHARACTERS, SETTING, EVENTS

Some of these words are _____

_____.

The tone the author creates with these words is _____

_____

because _____

_____.

[Repeat steps 1–3 if there are words that show a different tone and explain how the two tones are connected.]

_____

_____

_____

_____

What author's craft (like description, dialogue, internal dialogue, and gesture) does the author use in this [part of the story] and why do you think the author included it?

Name: _____ Date: _____

Steps to a great answer

1. Name the craft and the part of the text you are writing about.

2. Briefly describe what is happening in this part of the text.

3. Identify one example of this craft (quote or paraphrase) and explain what it shows.

4. Identify another example of this craft (quote or paraphrase) and explain what it shows.

5. [If there are other good examples, include them and explain what they show.]

6. Explain why you think the author used this craft in this part of the text.

In this part of _____

TITLE OF TEXT

one craft the author uses is_____.

Here is an example of this craft: _____

_____

_____.

This shows _____

_____.

Here is another example of this craft: _____

_____

_____

_____.

This shows _____

_____.

[If there are other examples, write them here.]

_____

_____

_____

_____

_____

_____

I think the author included this craft in this part of the story

because _____

_____

_____.

What figurative language (like simile, metaphor, personification, idiom, or hyperbole) does the author use in this [paragraph] and why do you think the author chose it?

Name: _____ **Date:** _____

Steps to a great answer

1. Identify the text and the kind of figurative language you found in the text.

2. Provide at least two examples from the text that show this figurative language.

3. Explain why you think the author included this figurative language.

4. [Repeat steps 1–3 if you find another kind of figurative language in the same passage.]

In this text, _____, one kind
TITLE OF TEXT
of figurative language the author used is _____

_____.

One example is _____

_____

_____.

Another example is _____

_____.

[Add more examples if you can find them.]

_____

_____

_____

_____

_____

_____.

I think the author chose to use this figurative language because ____

_____

_____

_____.

What elements of a [fable] did you find in this text? Find at least two elements and explain how the author uses them.

Name: _____ Date: _____

Steps to a great answer

1. Write a topic sentence that names the genre (in this case, a fable).

2. Name one element of a [fable] found in this story.

3. Show how the author uses this element in this story.

4. Name another element of a [fable] found in this story.

5. Show how the author uses this element in this story.

6. If there are more elements to identify and discuss, name the element and give a detail.

7. Explain why [fables] are an important genre.

The story _____
TITLE OF STORY
is a fable because it has several fable elements. One element is _____

_____.

Here is how the author shows this element in the story: _____

_____

_____

_____

_____

_____.

Another fable element in this story is _____

_____.

Here is how the author shows this element in the story: _____

_____

_____

_____

_____

_____.

Fables are an important genre because _____

_____

_____

_____.

Why do you think the author wrote this as a [poem]?

Name: _____ Date: _____

Steps to a great answer

1. Write a sentence that names the poem, what the poem is about, and its main message. (This might take two sentences.)

2. Write first about how the <u>language</u> of the writing is strong. (Consider descriptive words, personification, similes, and other examples of the way the author uses words.) Be sure to include quotes from the text to support your answer. For help, see Anchor Chart 21: Analyzing a Poem.

3. Now write about other features of the poem, the way it <u>looks</u> and the way it <u>sounds</u>.

4. End with how the poem makes *you* feel and *why*.

In the poem _____,
TITLE OF POEM
the author is writing about _____
_____.

The main message the author is trying to show is _____
_____.

The language makes this poem poetic in several ways. One way the author uses language is by including _____.
DESCRIPTIVE WORDS, SIMILES, OTHER
Here is an example: _____
_____
_____.

Another way the author uses language is by including _____

_____.

DESCRIPTIVE WORDS, SIMILES, OTHER

An example of this is _____

_____.

The <u>sound</u> and <u>look</u> of this poem also help the author share its message. Here is how the author does it: _____

_____

_____

_____.

This poem makes me feel _____

because _____

_____

_____.

What is this text feature and what is the most likely reason the author included it?

Name: _____ Date: _____

Steps to a great answer

1. Name the text feature.

2. Tell what the text feature shows.

3. Tell why the author probably included this text feature (how it adds to your understanding).

In the source, _____,
TITLE OF SOURCE

the text feature is _____.
NAME OF TEXT FEATURE

It shows _____

_____

_____

_____

_____.

I think the author included this text feature because _____

_____

_____

_____.

What text structure did the author choose for writing [about this topic] and what is the most likely reason the author chose it?

Name: _____   Date: _____

Steps to a great answer

1. Name the structure that the author used.

2. Explain how you know that this is the structure.

3. Give an example from the text that shows something about the structure.

4. Give another example from the text that shows something about the structure.

5. Explain why you think the author chose this structure to write about this topic.

The structure of this text, _____,
TITLE OF TEXT

is _____.

I think this is the structure because _____

_____

_____

_____

One example from the text that shows this structure is _____

_____

_____

_____

Another example from the text that shows this structure is _____

_____

_____

_____.

I think the author chose this structure because _____

_____

_____

_____.

What kind of information does the author provide in [paragraph A] and why does the author include it?

Name: _____ Date: _____

Steps to a great answer

1. Tell the *kind* of information the author is giving in this part of the text.

2. Explain how you know this is the *kind* of information.

3. Give at least one example that supports what the author is showing. (Give two examples if you can find two good ones.)

4. Explain *why* the author included this kind of information.

The kind of information the author is giving us in this paragraph is

_____

_____.

The author included this kind of information because _____

_____

_____

_____.

Here is one example: _____

_____

_____

_____.

Here is another example: _____

_____

_____

_____.

I think the author gave us this kind of information because _____

_____

_____

_____.

How does [paragraph A] connect to [paragraph B]?

Name: _____   **Date:** _____

Steps to a great answer

1. Name the two parts of the text you're writing about and tell how they are connected.

2. Show what you mean with a detail from [paragraph A].

3. Show what you mean with a detail from [paragraph B].

4. Explain why it was helpful (or not) for the author to connect these [paragraphs] in this way and *why*.

_____ [paragraph A] that begins
TITLE OF SOURCE

_____
WORDS FROM BEGINNING OF [PARAGRAPH A]

and [paragraph B] that begins _____
WORDS FROM BEGINNING OF [PARAGRAPH B]

_____

are connected by _____

_____.

A detail from [paragraph A] that shows this is _____

_____.

A detail from [paragraph B] that shows this is _____

_____

_____

_____.

I think it was helpful (or not helpful) that the author connected

these parts of the text this way because _____

_____

_____

_____.

Why did the author choose to begin/ end the story with this [paragraph]?

Name: _____ **Date:** _____

Steps to a great answer

1. Explain in one sentence how the author begins or ends the story.

2. Choose a detail from the beginning (or ending) to show what you mean.

3. If the author uses another technique to get readers into the story, explain what it is, and give an example.

4. Finish your answer by explaining why you do or do not think this was a good way to begin or end the story.

The author begins (ends) this story, _____,
　　　　　　　　　　　　　　　　　　　　　　TITLE OF SOURCE

by _____

_____

_____.

A detail that shows this is _____

_____

_____

_____.

Something else the author does at the beginning (end) of the story is

_____

_____

_____

_____ .

Here is a detail that shows this: _____

_____

_____

_____ .

I think this was a good way (not a good way) to start (or end) this story because _____

_____

_____ .

Where is the flashback in this story and why did the author most likely include it?

Name: _____ **Date:** _____

Steps to a great answer

1. Find the flashback. Explain how you know it's a flashback and what is happening in the flashback.

2. Decide what the flashback is trying to show.

3. Find at least two details in the flashback that prove what it is showing.

4. Explain why the author thought it was important to include the flashback.

There is a flashback in this story when _____

_____

_____

_____ .

This flashback shows that in the past _____

_____

_____

_____ .

For example, _____

_____

_____

_____ .

Another example was when _____

_____

_____

_____

_____.

It was important for the author to include this flashback because ____

_____

_____

_____

_____.

What is the backstory for this [story], and why did the author most likely include it?

Name: _____ Date: _____

Steps to a great answer

1. Explain in a few sentences what the story or news article is mainly about (a short summary).

2. Identify where the backstory is in the story or news article (probably either the beginning or end).

3. Explain the backstory in a summary of a few sentences.

4. Explain why the author probably included the backstory and why *you* think it is important.

In the main part of _____,
the author explains _____.

TITLE OF STORY OR NEWS ARTICLE

Here is what happens in this part of the story/article: _____

_____

_____

_____

_____

_____.

The author provides a backstory at the beginning/end of the text,
which explains _____

_____

_____

_____.

The author probably included this backstory because _____

_____

_____

_____.

I think it's important to have this background information because _

_____

_____

_____.

Why do you think the author included this quote from another author at the beginning of this [chapter]?

Name: _____ Date: _____

Steps to a great answer

1. In one sentence, explain the author's main reason for including this quote.

2. In your own words, explain what the quote means.

3. Give one or two details from the text itself to show how the quote connects to the book or chapter.

4. Explain why you think it was important to include this quote.

In _____, the author's main reason for
SOURCE
including this quote was to _____
_____.

The quote explains _____
_____
_____.

One detail from the text that shows this is_____
_____
_____
_____.

Another detail from the text that shows this is _____

_____

_____

_____.

I think it was important to include this quote because _____

_____

_____

_____.

How would this story change if it were told from [new narrator's] point of view?

Name: _____ **Date:** _____

Steps to a great answer

1. Begin with a sentence that names the new narrator and mentions that it would help you see this character's motivation, attitude, and feelings more clearly.

2. Write a sentence that names the motivation of the new narrator.

3. Choose a detail from the text that shows this motivation.

4. Write a sentence that names the attitude of the new narrator.

5. Choose a detail from the text that shows this attitude.

6. Write a sentence that names the feeling (or feelings) of the new narrator.

7. Choose a detail from the text that shows this feeling.

8. Explain why it might be good to tell this story from this character's point of view.

If _____, was told from

TITLE OF STORY

_____'s

CHARACTER'S NAME

point of view, it would more clearly show this character's motivation,

attitude, and feelings. You could see that this character was moti-

vated by _____.

A detail from the text that shows this motivation is _____

_____

_____

_____.

You could also see the character's attitude: _____

_____

_____

_____.

A detail from the text that shows this attitude is: _____

_____

_____

_____.

Finally, you could see this feeling: _____

_____.

A detail from the text that shows this feeling is: _____

_____

_____

_____.

It might be good to tell this story from _____ point
                                          NEW NARRATOR'S NAME
of view because _____

_____

_____.

What is your point of view about _____, and how is it the same or different from the point of view of the author?

Name: _____ Date: _____

Steps to a great answer

1. State the issue and your point of view about the issue.

2. State the main reason for your point of view.

3. Give one or more pieces of evidence to support this reason.

4. State another reason for your point of view.

5. Give one or more pieces of evidence to support this reason.

6. [Include other reasons and evidence to make your argument stronger.]

7. Explain why you disagree with the opposing point of view.

8. Explain why it is important to find a solution to this problem.

My point of view about _____

is _____

_____.

My most important reason for this is _____

_____.

Some evidence that supports this is _____

_____

_____

_____.

Another reason for my point of view is _____

_____.

Evidence that supports this is _____

_____

_____

_____.

Some people disagree with my point of view and think _____

_____

_____

_____.

I believe this is wrong because _____

_____

_____

_____.

It is important to solve this problem about _____

_____ because _____

_____

_____.

What was the author's purpose for including this [paragraph/sentence]?

Name: _____ Date: _____

Steps to a great answer

1. Identify the author's purpose for including this paragraph or sentence: *what* the author is doing.

2. Provide details from the paragraph or sentence that support this purpose.

3. Explain *why* the author wanted to include this information.

In this paragraph (or sentence), the author's purpose was to _____

_____

_____.

Some details from the paragraph (or sentence) are _____

_____

_____

_____

_____.

I think the author wanted to include _____

because _____

_____.

How did this video add to your understanding of _____?

Name: _____ Date: _____

Steps to a great answer

1. Identify the video and what it explains.

2. Briefly summarize the content of the video.

3. Identify the message and the images and other features of the video that make the message stronger.

4. Explain how these images and features add meaning to the words.

5. End by explaining why you think this video does (or does not) work well as a text.

This video, _____, explains _____
TITLE OF VIDEO
_____.

Here is a summary of what happens:_____

_____

_____

_____

_____

The message is_____

_____.

Different images and other features of the video help to make the

meaning stronger. For example: _____

_____

_____.

These images and features make the message stronger by _____

_____

_____.

Overall, I think this video works well as a text because _____

_____

_____.

Why do you think the author included this illustration (or photograph)?

Name: _____ **Date:** _____

Steps to a great answer

1. Identify the photograph or illustration you are describing and where it came from.

2. Briefly explain what the photograph or illustration shows.

3. Explain how the photograph or illustration makes you feel and why.

4. Explain why you think the author included this photograph or illustration.

5. Explain what you learned from the photograph or illustration that was not included in the print text that goes with it.

6. End with one (or more) points that could include: mood, colors, stereotypes, choice for cover, questions you still have, other.

This photograph (or illustration) of _____

TITLE OF SUBJECT OF PICTURE

comes from _____

_____.

It shows _____

_____

_____.

This picture makes me feel _____ because

_____

_____

_____.

I think the author included this picture because _____

_____

_____

_____.

This photograph (or illustration) adds to my understanding of this issue by _____

_____

_____.

One more thing I'd like to add from studying this photograph or illustration is _____

_____

_____.

Which details from [the text] are relevant to the argument that _____?

Name: _____ Date: _____

Steps to a great answer

1. Identify your source and the point you are defending.

2. Identify one relevant detail from the text and explain it.

3. Identify another relevant detail from the text and explain it.

4. If there are other relevant details, include them, too.

5. Explain why this topic is important.

In _____, the author writes about

TITLE OF SOURCE

_____.

One relevant detail that supports this is _____

_____

_____

_____.

Another relevant detail that supports this is _____

_____

_____

_____.

[If there are more relevant details, write about them here.]

_____

_____

_____

_____

_____

_____.

This topic is important because _____

_____

_____

_____.

What additional evidence for _____ could the author have included to make the argument more convincing?

Name: _____ **Date:** _____

Steps to a great answer

1. Write an introductory sentence that identifies the topic and what the author is arguing for.

2. Write a sentence or two about the relevant evidence the author has already provided.

3. Identify an additional kind of evidence the author could have included and how it would be helpful.

4. Identify at least one more kind of evidence the author could have included and how it would be helpful.

5. Write a wrap-up sentence that describes how the added evidence would have made the author's argument stronger.

In this [article], the author argued for _____

_____.

Some relevant evidence the author provided to support this was _____

_____

_____

_____

_____

_____.

Another kind of evidence the author could have included was _____

_____.

This could have been helpful because _____

_____

_____

_____.

One more kind of evidence the author could have included was _____

_____.

This could have been helpful because _____

_____

_____

_____.

This evidence would make the author's argument stronger because

_____

_____

_____.

Which source does a better job of explaining _____? Cite specific evidence to support your answer.

Name: _____ **Date:** _____

Steps to a great answer

1. Identify the source that provides a better (clearer and more thorough) explanation.

2. Explain *why* this explanation is better (clearer and more thorough).

3. Give an example (or two) from the text.

4. Tell why the explanation in the other source is not as clear or thorough.

5. Give an example (or two) from the text.

6. Explain why this difference in sources is important.

The source that provides the best explanation of _____

_____
WHAT IS THE SOURCE EXPLAINING?

is _____.
TITLE OF STRONGER SOURCE

It is clearer because _____

_____

_____

Here is an example: _____

_____

_____

_____.

The explanation in the other source, _____

is not as clear because _____

_____.

Here is an example: _____

_____

_____

_____

_____.

This difference in sources is important because _____

_____

_____

_____.

Explain how each of the selections you read about [topic] could be useful to someone writing about this topic.

Name: _____ **Date:** _____

Steps to a great answer

1. Write an introductory sentence that states the big idea of both sources.

2. Write about <u>key words</u> you would identify, defined or explained in both sources.

3. Write about the <u>facts</u> you would include from both sources.

4. Write about <u>stories</u> you would include from the sources that would make your writing interesting.

5. Write a sentence or two about what you would include in a conclusion about this topic.

*Both _____ and
SOURCE 1

_____
SOURCE 2

include information about _____

_____.

If I was writing a report about this information, I would include

important <u>words</u> defined in these sources such as _____

_____.

I would include these important <u>facts</u> from both sources: _____

_____

_____

_____

_____.

I would include these <u>quotes</u> from experts: _____

_____

_____

_____.

These quotes show _____

_____.

To make this topic seem more real, I would include this <u>story or</u>

<u>example</u> from _____.
                                     TITLE OF SOURCE
It shows _____

_____.

My conclusion would show that this topic is important because _____

_____

_____

_____.

*This frame may need to be modified depending on the evidence in each source. Always indicate the title of the source where you located a piece of evidence.

Use the information from these [two] sources to write a diary entry from your point of view, imagining that you are personally experiencing the situation identified in these sources. Be sure to include details from the informational sources you read.

Name: _____   **Date:** _____

Steps to a great answer

1. Include the date and a <u>greeting</u> at the beginning of your response.

2. In a sentence or two, tell what has been <u>happening</u>.

3. Include your <u>feelings</u> about these events.

4. Include some <u>opinions</u> about these events.

5. End with a <u>closing</u> that includes your name.

Date of your diary entry

Dear Diary,

Here is what has been happening in my life recently_____

_____

_____

_____

_____

_____.

All of this makes me feel _____ because

_____

_____

_____.

In my opinion _____

_____

_____

_____

_____

_____.

Your friend, _____

Identify the central idea in Source #1 and Source #2. Then compare and contrast the way the author develops the central idea in each of the sources.

Name: _____ Date: _____

Steps to a great answer

1. Decide the <u>topic</u> that works for <u>both</u> sources and then determine your central idea.

2. First paragraph: Write an introduction that names the <u>central idea</u> (message) and states something important that is <u>similar</u> about both sources, or something that is <u>different</u>.

3. Second paragraph: Write about the <u>first source</u>, showing how the author <u>developed the central idea</u>. Include details, and a quote if possible.

4. Third paragraph: Write about the <u>second source</u>, showing how the author <u>developed the central idea.</u> Include details, and a quote if possible.

5. Final paragraph: Explain <u>why this central idea is important</u>.

Paragraph 1: Introduction

In Source #1, _____, and in Source #2

TITLE OF SOURCE #1

_____,

TITLE OF SOURCE #2

the central idea is _____

_____.

These sources are <u>similar/different</u> because _____
CHOOSE ONE

_____

_____

_____

_____.

Paragraph 2:

What happens in Source #1 that shows this central idea?

Here is what happens in Source #1, _____:
TITLE OF SOURCE #1

_____

_____

_____

_____

_____

_____

Paragraph 3:

What happens in Source #2 that shows this central idea?

Here is what happens in Source #2, _____:
TITLE OF SOURCE #2

_____

_____

_____

_____

_____

_____

Final Paragraph: Explain the importance

It is important for me to remember this lesson because _____

_____

_____.

Appendix

Study Guide with Suggested Resources:

Teaching Practices That Lead to Awesome Answers

While student work (in this case constructed response) is the "bottom line," the evidence that dictates the course of our next instructional steps, we also know that our teaching practices have contributed to students' performance. When we see that certain issues are trends among several students rather than isolated problems faced by one or two individuals, we wonder what we could have done differently to yield better results. Reflecting systematically on our instruction may help us recognize small changes to our practice that could have a big impact on student outcomes.

To support meaningful reflection, I've identified 10 teacher practices to maximize students' competency with both analytical reading and constructed response. Each of the 10 points, which you will recognize from Part I, is reviewed briefly. I've also suggested related readings for all areas, both online and print resources—just right for individual contemplation or professional study with colleagues. Finally, a checklist matched to the 10 practices is provided for self-reflection: Reflecting on Teacher Practices That Enhance Students' Analytical Reading and Constructed Response.

How powerful would it be to contemplate some of these reflection points with colleagues! Form a study group, find a critical friend, ask a coach for support. And prioritize. One of the mistakes we make over and over as teachers is to try to do it all. Right now. Today. Instead, choose one or two areas identified on the Teacher Practices checklist and for the moment, focus only on those.

Then choose a concept and a question to apply your prioritized practices. The good news is that there are plenty of classroom-ready resources and instructional strategies in Parts II and III of this book that will save you time by offering at-your-fingertips tools to get started. I mentioned earlier that I love comprehension questions. In this book, I've done all I can to help you and your students understand these questions, and just possibly to love them, too.

Ten Points for Teacher Reflection

1. Provide instruction in analytical reading and constructed response within a structure that maximizes student engagement and teacher monitoring.

The virtual lesson described in Chapter 1 was presented to a small group. I do not claim that analytical reading and writing can *only* be taught in small groups. But my decision to teach this lesson to only a few students was intentional. Often when I visit schools, I teach a whole class lesson (for example, when I'm *introducing* a concept in close reading or author's craft or focusing on social emotional learning). But in this case, I wanted to elicit as much student interaction as possible in a setting that students would view as low risk. I wanted to monitor performance thoroughly for every student in the group, and promote as much progress as possible for everyone. Additionally, all students in this group had a common instructional need that our lesson focus would address. How do you decide when small group instruction is the best format? How do you determine the composition of your groups? For more perspective regarding small group instruction, see these sources:

- Duke, N. K. (2019, July). Turn small reading groups into big wins. *ASCD Education Update. 61*(7). Retrieved from http://www.ascd.org/publications/ newsletters/education-update/jul19/vol61/num07/Turn-Small-Reading-Groups-into-Big-Wins.aspx
- 4 benefits of small group reading instruction. (2017, March 1). 4imprint. Retrieved from https://info.4imprint.com/enews/4-benefits-small-group-instruction/
- Shanahan, T. (2018, April 28). Whole class or small group. [Blog post]. Retrieved from https://shanahanonliteracy.com/blog/should-reading-be-taught-whole -class-or-small-group

2. Include reading selections that are both literary and informational, of a length and level of complexity that support students' growth as readers and writers.

We want students to read texts of all lengths, but when we're teaching a process like summarizing or determining theme and need to access a full text for the process to make sense, a short selection is perfect. We have many options available: short stories, poems, informational articles, essays, song lyrics … the list goes on. Similarly, we want to be aware of the complexity of the text, recognizing that *all* students should have access to challenging sources—along with the kind of instruction that helps them navigate complexity. Where do you look for short, appropriately complex text? For more perspective regarding text length and complexity, see these sources:

- Klein, A. (2016, June 30). The compelling why: Using short texts to teach close reading. [Blog post]. Retrieved from https://edublog.scholastic.com/post/compelling-why-using-short-texts-support-close-reading#
- Lemov, D. (2015, September 28). The particular benefits of short stories. [Blog post]. Retrieved from https://teachlikeachampion.com/blog/particular-benefits-short-stories/
- Common Core State Standards for English Language Arts and Literacy in History/Social Studies, Science and Technical Subjects: Appendix A: Elements Supporting Key Elements of the Standards. (n.d.) Retrieved from http://www.corestandards.org/assets/Appendix_A.pdf

3. Pose questions aligned to a full range of standards and expected rigor.

If there's anything we can do to support students' comprehension, this is it: Ask questions across a full range of standards. Even *exposure* to questions without explicitly teaching response strategies is a step in the right direction. Let students hear questions for all standards, especially questions you've never asked before. Let them hear you model the way you'd answer these questions and facilitate conversations with their peers in which they discuss answers together. Make sure your questions not only address all standards, but also deeper thinking about standards. If you ask a question to check for basic understanding, then ask a follow-up question that requires an inference. What new questions have you asked recently? What new question could you ask? How are you reinforcing deeper thinking? For more perspective regarding Depth of Knowledge, standards-based questions, and questioning techniques, see these sources:

- Boyles, N. (2018). *Reading, writing, and rigor: Helping students achieve greater depth of knowledge in literacy.* Alexandria, VA: ASCD.
- Center for Innovation in Teaching and Learning. (n.d.). Questioning strategies. Retrieved from https://citl.illinois.edu/citl-101/teaching-learning/resources/teaching-strategies/questioning-strategies
- Daiber, R., Garrett, K., Kasselbaum, M., Davis, K., Pfeiffer, L., Sarfaty, S., & Wollerman, J. (n.d.). Text-dependent questions reflecting Common Core Standards for reading by grade level: Elementary. Retrieved from http://www.stclair.k12.il.us/ccore/ELAShifts/documents/Text%20Based%20Questions/CCSS%20for%20Reading%20Elementary.pdf

4. **Require students to make inferences, cite evidence, and explain importance when answering questions.**

Different questions require different response strategies, but all of them require evidence, and most entail both an inference and an explanation of importance. The virtual lesson addressed a question that involved all three of these criteria (and more because it also entailed comparing texts). What questions are you asking that address these three very basic components? What are the most common areas of difficulty? How are you addressing these needs? For more perspective on elements of a constructed response, see these sources:

- Teach constructed response writing explicitly. (2013, August 27). [Blog post]. Retrieved from https://www.smekenseducation.com/teach-constructedresponse -writi/
- Constructed response questions. (n.d.). 240 Tutoring, Inc. Retrieved from https://www.240tutoring.com/constructed-response-questions/
- Findley, J. (2018, February 23). Tips for teaching RACE constructed response strategy. [Blog post]. Retrieved from https://jenniferfindley.com/tips-for-teaching -race-constructed-response-strategy/

5. **Analyze the literacy task ahead of instruction and be proactive about addressing potential areas of difficulty before they negatively impact student learning.**

We often make assumptions during literacy instruction that students are ready for a next instructional step, and then feel frustrated when they don't "get it." We need to get better at anticipating places where learning will go off-track and then be proactive about addressing these issues *before* students fail. What is there about the text you are reading with your students that could confuse them? Do they need to compare characters? If so, do they understand what to look for when comparing characters? Do they need to choose evidence selectively? If so, what do we consider when making decisions about the *best* evidence? In short, how well are you anticipating (and planning for) students' needs in textual analysis? For more perspective on textual analysis in literary and informational text, see these resources:

- Robb, L. (2016). *Read, talk, write: 35 lessons that teach students to analyze fiction and nonfiction*. Thousand Oaks, CA: Corwin.
- Kinsella, K. (n.d.). Cutting to the common core: Informational text analysis. Language Magazine. Retrieved from https://www.languagemagazine.com/ cutting-to-the-common-core-analyzing-informational-text/
- Arubail, R. (2014, December 3). Teaching literary analysis. [Blog post]. Retrieved from https://www.edutopia.org/blog/reaching-literary-analysis-rusul-alrubail

6. **Provide opportunities for student discourse as a means of increasing understanding.**

In any literacy discussion, students should be doing more talking than the teacher. How do you make sure that it's students' voices that dominate? Do all students participate? How do you get reluctant talkers to join in? Do they build on each other's responses to shape their thinking and truly listen to each other? What do you learn from students' conversations that helps you better understand how they think, and what you could do to promote even better thinking? For more perspective on the impact of student discussions and how to promote good discussions, see these sources:

- Mulvahill, E. (2018, November 2). Why kids need more talk time in the classroom. [Blog post]. Retrieved from https://www.weareteachers.com/talk-time-in-the-classroom/
- Mendler, A. (2013, November 5). Teaching your students how to have a conversation. [Blog post]. Retrieved from https://www.edutopia.org/blog/teaching-your-students-conversation-allen-mendler
- Kuper, L. (2016, September 7). How to use classroom conversation to improve learning. [Blog post]. Retrieved from https://www.theguardian.com/teacher-network/2016/sep/07/how-to-classroom-conversation-can

7. **Provide scaffolds such as anchor charts, checklists, oral rehearsal cue cards, and answer frames to support students' reading and writing as needed.**

There are many ways we can scaffold students as they become better equipped to handle the challenges of constructed response. But, remember that things like anchor charts, cue cards, and answer frames *follow* instruction. They are not a substitute for the instruction itself. If you are using one of the anchor charts in this book or any of the hands-on supports, what teacher-moves preceded this step? How did you know students were ready for oral rehearsal? How did you decide who should use the answer frame to write their answer, and who would do just as well with a blank piece of paper? For more perspective regarding scaffolding with graphic support, see these sources:

- Integrating language and content: Creating sentence frames. [PowerPoint slides]. Retrieved from https://dcps.duvalschools.org/site/handlers/filedownload.ashx?moduleinstanceid=23794&dataid=25636&FileName=Creating%20Sentence%20Frames.pdf
- Ferlazzo, L. (2016, December 1). The best scaffolded writing frames for students. [Blog post]. https://larryferlazzo.edublogs.org/2016/12/01/the-best-scaffolded-writing-frames-for-students/

- Center for English Learners. (2018, December). Exhibit 6. Prompt and response frames for supporting academic conversations. Retrieved from https://www .air.org/sites/default/files/Danielson-Exhibit-6-Prompt-and-Response-Frames .pdf

8. Apply principles of explicit instruction that demonstrate the gradual release of responsibility leading to student independence.

The virtual lesson in Chapter 1 demonstrated explicit instruction in action. There was an explanation of the goal and how we would achieve it (examining the anchor chart for Topics and Central Ideas). I modeled oral rehearsal before students practiced themselves. Then they moved closer to independence by writing their own response using an answer frame. At the end, we reflected on what we had learned. While principles of explicit instruction were evident in this lesson, and there was some gradual release, there would need to be more lessons and more practice for students to achieve real independence. What are you doing to honor each component of explicit instruction within your lessons? How are you systematically moving students toward independence over time so that each day they have a bit more independence than they had the previous day? For more perspective regarding explicit instruction and the gradual release of responsibility, see these resources:

- Levy, E. (n.d.). Gradual release of responsibility: I do, we do, you do. E.L. Achieve/2007. Retrieved from https://familiesaspartners.org/wp-content/ uploads/I-do-You-do-We-do.pdf
- Greene, K. (n.d.). Explicit instruction: What you need to know. Understood for All, Inc. Retrieved from https://www.understood.org/en/school-learning/ for-educators/universal-design-for-learning/what-is-explicit-instruction
- Texas Education Agency (n.d.). What is effective comprehension instruction? *Reading Rockets*. Retrieved from https://www.readingrockets.org/article/ what-effective-comprehension-instruction

9. Provide feedback to students regarding their progress in analytical reading and constructed response to help them set their own literacy goals.

We know that feedback is important to students. The best feedback is specific, as immediate as possible, and helps students recognize progress toward their goal. For the virtual lesson, working with students in a small group contributed to meeting all three of these criteria. I could monitor students as they rehearsed their response orally, then wrote it, providing both encouragement and guidance. Because we were "in the moment," students were able to use suggestions (and moral support) to push forward.

How immediate is your feedback? Does it clarify the fine points? Does it move students closer to their goal? For more perspective on feedback, see these sources:

- Stenger, M. (2014, August 6). Five research-based tips for providing students with meaningful feedback. [Blog post]. Retrieved from https://www.edutopia.org/blog/tips-providing-students-meaningful-feedback-marianne-stenger
- The importance of feedback for student learning. (2019, January 8). [Blog post]. Retrieved from https://www.thegraidenetwork.com/blog-all/importance-of-feedback-student-learning
- Wiggins, G. (2012). Seven keys to effective feedback. *Educational Leadership*, *70*(1), 10–16.

10. **Use student performance data, including constructed responses, to determine next instructional steps.**

In some ways, all instruction is assessment. We analyze students' performance today to determine what we'll teach tomorrow—which was certainly the case in our virtual lesson. At the end of that session, two points were clear. First, students' awareness of the response process was not as solid as I had hoped. They could perform the steps, but had a hard time repeating them back to me. Tomorrow that would need to be a priority: recognizing the logic of the steps involved. What *did* work out well was students' written responses with the support of an answer frame. I would take a closer look at their responses later, but it was possible some students would be encouraged *not* to use the frame in the next lesson. How do you reflect on today's lesson outcomes to inform tomorrow's instruction? For more perspective on using data formatively, see these resources:

- Skauge, T. (2019, June 3). Using formative assessment data to guide learning. [Blog post]. Retrieved from https://www.edmentuminternational.com/blog/using-formative-assessment-data-to-guide-learning/
- Wilson, E. (2016, March 6). Five ways of using formative assessment for actionable data. [Blog post]. Retrieved from https://www.edmentuminternational.com/blog/using-formative-assessment-data-to-guide-learning/
- Dyer, K. (2018, May 29). Formative instructional practice—Using the results and data are what matters. [Blog post]. Retrieved from https://www.nwea.org/blog/2018/formative-instructional-practice-using-the-results-and-data-are-what-matters/

REFLECTING ON TEACHER PRACTICES THAT ENHANCE STUDENTS' ANALYTICAL READING AND CONSTRUCTED RESPONSE

Teacher _____ **Date** _____

☐ I provide instruction in analytical reading and constructed response within a structure that maximizes student engagement and teacher monitoring.

☐ I choose texts that are both literary and informational of a length and level of complexity that support students' growth as readers and writers.

☐ I pose questions aligned to a full range of standards and expected rigor.

☐ I require students to make inferences, cite evidence, and explain importance when answering questions.

☐ I analyze the literacy task ahead of instruction and am proactive about addressing potential areas of difficulty before they negatively impact student learning.

☐ I provide opportunities for student discourse as a means of increasing student understanding.

☐ I provide scaffolds such as anchor charts, checklists, oral rehearsal cue cards, and answer frames to support students' reading and writing as needed.

☐ I apply principles of explicit instruction that demonstrate the gradual release of responsibility leading to student independence.

☐ I provide feedback to students regarding their progress in analytical reading and constructed response to help them set their own literacy goals.

☐ I use student performance data including constructed responses to determine next instructional steps.

My area(s) of greatest strength:

An area in which I would like to grow:

Questions I still have:

BIBLIOGRAPHY OF PROFESSIONAL RESOURCES

4 benefits of small group reading instruction. (2017, March 1). 4imprint. Retrieved from https://info.4imprint.com/enews/4-benefits-small-group-instruction/

Arubail, R. (2014, December 3). Teaching literary analysis. [Blog post]. Retrieved from https://www.edutopia.org/blog/reaching-literary-analysis-rusul-alrubail

Boyles, N. (2018). *Reading, writing, and rigor: Helping students achieve greater depth of knowledge in literacy.* Alexandria, VA: ASCD.

Center for English Learners. (2018, December). Exhibit 6. Prompt and response frames for supporting academic conversations. Retrieved from https://www.air.org/sites/default/files/Danielson-Exhibit-6-Prompt-and-Response-Frames.pdf

Center for Innovation in Teaching and Learning. (n.d.). Questioning strategies. Retrieved from https://citl.illinois.edu/citl-101/teaching-learning/resources/teaching-strategies/questioning-strategies

Common Core State Standards for English Language Arts and Literacy in History/Social Studies, Science and Technical Subjects: Appendix A: Elements Supporting Key Elements of the Standards. (n.d.). Retrieved from http://www.corestandards.org/assets/Appendix_A.pdf

Constructed response questions. (n.d.). 240 Tutoring, Inc. Retrieved from https://www.240tutoring.com/constructed-response-questions/

Daiber, R., Garrett, K., Kasselbaum, M., Davis, K., Pfeiffer, L., Sarfaty, S., & Wollerman, J. (n.d.). Text-dependent questions reflecting Common Core Standards for reading by grade level: Elementary. Retrieved from http://www.stclair.k12.il.us/ccore/ELAShifts/documents/Text%20Based%20Questions/CCSS%20for%20Reading%20Elementary.pdf

Duke, N. K. (2019, July). Turn small reading groups into big wins. *ASCD Education Update. 61*(7). Retrieved from http://www.ascd.org/publications/newsletters/education-update/jul19/vol61/num07/Turn-Small-Reading-Groups-into-Big-Wins.aspx

Dyer, K. (2018, May 29). Formative instructional practice—Using the results and data are what matters. [Blog post]. Retrieved from https://www.nwea.org/blog/2018/formative-instructional-practice-using-the-results-and-data-are-what-matters/

Ferlazzo, L. (2016, December 1). The best scaffolded writing frames for students. [Blog post]. https://larryferlazzo.edublogs.org/2016/12/01/the-best-scaffolded-writing-frames-for-students/

Findley, J. (2018, February 23). Tips for teaching RACE constructed response strategy. [Blog post]. Retrieved from https://jenniferfindley.com/tips-for-teaching-race-constructed-response-strategy/

Greene, K. (n.d.). Explicit instruction: What you need to know. Understood for All, Inc. Retrieved from https://www.understood.org/en/school-learning/for-educators/universal-design-for-learning/what-is-explicit-instruction

The importance of feedback for student learning. (2019, January 8). [Blog post]. Retrieved from https://www.thegraidenetwork.com/blog-all/importance-of-feedback-student-learning

Integrating language and content: Creating sentence frames. [PowerPoint slides]. Retrieved from https://dcps.duvalschools.org/site/handlers/filedownload.ashx?moduleinstanceid=23794&dataid=25636&FileName=Creating%20Sentence%20Frames.pdf

Kinsella, K. (n.d.) Cutting to the common core: Informational text analysis. *Language Magazine*. Retrieved from https://www.languagemagazine.com/cutting-to-the-common-core-analyzing-informational-text/

Klein, A. (2016, June 30). The compelling why: Using short texts to teach close reading. [Blog post]. Retrieved from https://edublog.scholastic.com/post/compelling-why-using-short-texts-support-close-reading#

Kuper, L. (2016, September 7). How to use classroom conversation to improve learning. [Blog post]. Retrieved from https://www.theguardian.com/teacher-network/2016/sep/07/how-to-classroom-conversation-can

Lemov, D. (2015, September 28). The particular benefits of short stories. [Blog post]. Retrieved from https://teachlikeachampion.com/blog/particular-benefits-short-stories/

Levy, E. (n.d.). Gradual release of responsibility: I do, we do, you do. E.L. Achieve/2007. Retrieved from https://familiesaspartners.org/wp-content/uploads/I-do-You-do-We-do.pdf

Mendler, A. (2013, November 5). Teaching your students how to have a conversation. [Blog post]. Retrieved from https://www.edutopia.org/blog/teaching-your-students-conversation-allen-mendler

Mulvahill, E. (2018, November 2). Why kids need more talk time in the classroom. [Blog post]. Retrieved from https://www.weareteachers.com/talk-time-in-the-classroom/

Robb, L. (2016). *Read, talk, write: 35 lessons that teach students to analyze fiction and nonfiction*. Thousand Oaks, CA: Corwin.

Shanahan, T. (2018, April 28). Whole class or small group. [Blog post]. Retrieved from https://shanahanonliteracy.com/blog/should-reading-be-taught-whole-class-or-small-group

Skauge, T. (2019, June 3). Using formative assessment data to guide learning. [Blog post]. Retrieved from https://www.edmentuminternational.com/blog/using-formative-assessment-data-to-guide-learning/

Stenger, M. (2014, August 6). Five research-based tips for providing students with meaningful feedback. [Blog post]. Retrieved from https://www.edutopia.org/blog/tips-providing-students-meaningful-feedback-marianne-stenger

Teach constructed response writing explicitly. (2013, August 27). [Blog post]. Retrieved from https://www.smekenseducation.com/teach-constructedresponse-writi/

Texas Education Agency (n.d.). What is effective comprehension instruction? *Reading Rockets*. Retrieved from https://www.readingrockets.org/article/what-effective-comprehension-instruction

Wilson, E. (2016, March 6). Five ways of using formative assessment for actionable data. [Blog post]. Retrieved from https://elearningindustry.com/5-ways-using-formative-assessment-actionable-data

Wiggins, G. (2012). Seven keys to effective feedback. *Educational Leadership*, 70(1), 10–16.

BIBLIOGRAPHY OF READING SELECTIONS FOR SAMPLE RESPONSES

Aesop (2006). The bees and wasps, and the hornet. Project Gutenberg. Retrieved from https://www.gutenberg.org/files/19994/19994-h/19994-h.htm#Page_56

Aesop. (2006). The fox and the stork. Project Gutenberg. Retrieved from https://www.gutenberg.org/files/19994/19994-h/19994-h.htm#Page_56

Aesop. (2006). Mercury and the woodman. Project Gutenberg. Retrieved from https://www.gutenberg.org/files/19994/19994-h/19994-h.htm#Page_73

Aesop. (2006). The old lion and the fox. Project Gutenberg. Retrieved from https://www.gutenberg.org/files/19994/19994-h/19994-h.htm#Page_34

Aesop. (2008). The ant and the dove. (G.F. Townsend, Trans.). Project Gutenberg. Retrieved from https://www.gutenberg.org/files/21/21-h/21-h.htm#link2H_4_0289

Aesop. (2008). The lion and the mouse. (G.F. Townsend, Trans.)Retrieved from https://www.gutenberg.org/files/21/21-h/21-h.htm#link2H_4_0004

Applegate, K. (2014). *Ivan: The remarkable true story of the shopping mall gorilla.* New York: Clarion Books.

The ballad of Birmingham. (2015, December 11). [Video file]. Retrieved from https://youtu.be/JXpOI8WSiBo

Barrie, J.M. (2008). Peter breaks through. *Peter Pan* (Ch. 1). Retrieved from http://www.gutenberg.org/files/16/16-h/16-h.htm

Barrie, J.M. (2008). Come away, come away. *Peter Pan* (Ch. 3). Retrieved from http://www.gutenberg.org/files/16/16-h/16-h.htm#link2HCH0003

China today—China's population. (n.d.) ReadWorks. Retrieved from https://www.readworks.org/article/China-Today---Chinas-Population/31b0af8d-5a48-43f2-b036-0bf8e16ccade#!articleTab:content/

Civil rights on a city bus. (n.d). ReadWorks. Retrieved from https://www.readworks.org/article/Civil-Rights-on-a-City-Bus/b4eecc45-7efc-4e0c-a759-87807b9e3bae#!articleTab:content/

Coles, R. (2010). *The story of Ruby Bridges.* New York: Scholastic.

Colson, A. (2018). *Unstoppable: How Jim Thorpe and the Carlisle Indian School football team defeated Army.* Mankato, MN: Capstone Publishers.

The Continental Army at Valley Forge, 1777. (2006). EyeWitness to History. Retrieved from http://www.eyewitnesstohistory.com/valleyforge.htm

Cooper, G. (2005). October's party. Retrieved from https://www.amblesideonline.org/AOPoemsOct.shtml#oct01

Cooper, G. (2005). The wind and the leaves. In W. H. McGuffey (Ed.), *McGuffey's Second Eclectic Reader.* Retrieved from https://www.gutenberg.org/files/14668/14668.txt

Dolasia, M. (2020, February 11). NASA engineers fix glitch on Voyager 2 spacecraft from 11.5 billion miles away! Retrieved from https://www.dogonews.com/2020/2/11/nasa-engineers-fix-glitch-on-voyager-2-spacecraft-from-11-dot-5-billion-miles-away

Gehrig, L. (1939). *Farewell to baseball address.* American Rhetoric: Top 100 Speeches. Retrieved from https://americanrhetoric.com/speeches/lougehrigfarewelltobaseball.htm

Hoose, H., & Hoose, P. (1998). *Hey little ant.* Berkeley, CA: Tricycle Press.

Markarian, M. (n.d.). Taking down the green-eyed monster. ReadWorks. Retrieved from http://www.readworks.org/passages/taking-down-green-eyed-monster

McClure, L. (n.d.). A chance for freedom. ReadWorks. Retrieved from https://www.readworks.org/article/A-Chance-for-Freedom/98c9875c-6cbb-4db3-86ea-56ddcb15d8bf#!articleTab:content/

National Geographic Kids. (n.d.). Amazing animals: Gorilla. [Video file]. Retrieved from https://kids.nationalgeographic.com/videos/amazing-animals/#/455626819925

News debate: Cash courses. (n.d.). ReadWorks. Retrieved from https://www.readworks.org/article/News-Debate-Cash-Courses/df0ae883-8d82-4f5d-9b3b-e371b864ed8d#!articleTab:content/

News debate: Snowed out! (n.d.). ReadWorks. Retrieved from https://www.readworks.org/article/News-Debate-Snowed-Out!/991d4949-f5ed-4c0a-bd3e-cf420189fcc8#!articleTab:content/

Olson, M.B. (2012). Best friends. In *Chicken soup for the kid's soul*. New York: Simon and Schuster. 63–65.

[Photograph of destruction from the bomb and pictures of the four young girls killed in the Birmingham church bombing]. (1963). Retrieved from https://www.google.com/search?tbm=isch&sxsrf=ALeKk00HIBtbl5c5wiKBy5-lJs1I377MUg%3A1587492296232&source=hp&biw=1280&bih=578&ei=yDWfXo6qC-HB_Qbi37OQAQ&q=birminghamchurch+bombing&oq=birmingham&gs_lcp=CgNpbWcQARgAMgIIxAnMgIIADICCAAyAggAMgIIADICCAAyAggAMgIIADICCAAyAggAOgcIIxDqAhAnOgUIABCDAVDpEFjTHWChLGgCcAB4AIABYogBhQaSAQIxMJgBAKABAaoBC2d3cy13aXotaW1nAEK&sclient=img#imgrc=wYrDJuZg74gKRM

Prelutsky. J. (2013). The new kid on the block. In *The new kid on the block*. New York: Green Willow Books.

Randall, D. (1965). The ballad of Birmingham. All Poetry. Retrieved from https://allpoetry.com/Ballad-Of-Birmingham

The Revolutionary War: Valley Forge. (n.d.). ReadWorks. Retrieved from https://www.readworks.org/article/The-American-Revolutionary-War/bd014cce-fbb2-4a72-bc91-d4598ae251b9#!articleTab:content/contentSection:0e0d24c0-8514-42de-b9a3-8b94de36a06f/

Robinson, S. (2009). *Testing the ice: A true story about Jackie Robinson*. New York: Scholastic.

Rylant, C. (1985). Spaghetti. In *Every living thing*. New York: Simon and Schuster.

Sherwood, K.B. (n.d.). Molly pitcher. Project Gutenberg. Retrieved from https://www.gutenberg.org/files/47476/47476-h/47476-h.htm

Slavery, Civil War & reconstruction—The Underground Railroad. (n.d.). ReadWorks. Retrieved from https://www.readworks.org/article/Slavery-Civil-War-Reconstruction---The-Underground-Railroad/d72ef095-19e7-41d3-916d-1e27803e75ea#!articleTab:content/

Spyri, J. (1881). Up the mountains to Alm-Uncle. *Heidi* (Ch. 1). Retrieved from http://www.gutenberg.org/cache/epub/1448/pg1448-images.html

Stevenson, R.L. (2008). Block city. In *A child's garden of verses*. Retrieved from http://www.gutenberg.org/cache/epub/136/pg136-images.html

Stevenson, R.L. (2008). The land of nod. In *A child's garden of verses*. Retrieved from http://www.gutenberg.org/files/25617/25617-h/25617-h.htm

SummerReads: Bikes & boards—catch a wave. (n.d.). ReadWorks. Retrieved from https://www.readworks.org/article/SummerReads-Bikes-Boards-Catch-a-Wave/4c050feb-222d-4bd1-8c81-f88d0cea4cce#!articleTab:content/

The tale of the barnacle and the whale. (n.d.). ReadWorks. Retrieved https://www.readworks.org/article/Relationships-between-Living-Things/e9f6b90b-9b6b-4d1a-9fa8-c16409ddad76#!articleTab:content/contentSection:089f3043-2d12-4cd1-bb4f-6251db583334/

Tiger attack spurs debate. (n.d.). ReadWorks. Retrieved from https://www.readworks.org/article/Debate-Are-Zoos-Bad-News/78fe932f-70a9-42e9-9e91-7e951f0a8ba8#!articleTab:content/

Tobin, D. (2020). Fun facts bout The Oregon Trail for kids. American History for Kids. Retrieved from https://www.americanhistoryforkids.com/the-oregon-trail/

The two Harriets, heroines of abolition. (n.d.). ReadWorks. Retrieved from https://www.readworks.org/article/The-Two-Harriets-Heroines-of-Abolition/893243b9-225b-42d7-b390-62aaa5315dc3#!articleTab:content/

Van Allsburg, C. (1986). *The stranger.* Boston, MA: Houghton Mifflin Harcourt.

Westward expansion—The Oregon Trail. (n.d.). ReadWorks. Retrieved from https://www.americanhistoryforkids.com/the-oregon-trail/

White, E. B. (2007). *Some pig!: A Charlotte's web picture book.* New York: Harper Collins.

Williams, M. (2004). *The velveteen rabbit.* Project Gutenberg. Retrieved from http://www.gutenberg.org/files/11757/11757-h/11757-h.htm

The woolly mammoth. (n.d.). Retrieved from https://www.readworks.org/article/The-Woolly-Mammoth/adbf8219-0401-4b8f-af36-39caf8aa5f5d#!articleTab:content/

INDEX OF INSTRUCTIONAL RESOURCES

Question 2.3: What is the central idea/theme of _____ and how does the author develop it?

Question 2.4: What is the main idea of this [paragraph] and how does the author develop it?

Question 2.5: Briefly summarize this story including only the key points.

Question 2.6: What conclusion can you draw about [character, problem, etc.]?

Question 3.1: What character trait (or feeling) does [character] mostly show in this story (or in this part of the story)?

Question 4.4: What author's craft (like description, dialogue, internal dialogue, and gesture) does the author use in this [part of the story] and why do you think the author included it?

Question 4.5: What figurative language (like simile, metaphor, personification, idiom, or hyperbole) does the author use in this [paragraph] and why do you think the author chose it?

Question 4.6: What elements of a [fable] did you find in this text? Find at least two elements and explain how the author uses them.

Question 4.7: Why do you think the author wrote this as a [poem]?

Question 5.1: What is this text feature and what is the most likely reason the author included it?

Question 5.2: What text structure did the author choose for writing [about this topic] and what is the most likely reason the author chose it?

Question 5.3: What kind of information does the author provide in [paragraph A] and why does the author include it?

Question 5.4: How does [paragraph A] connect to [paragraph B]?

Question 5.5: Why did the author choose to begin/end the story with this [paragraph]?

Question 9.4: Identify the central idea in Source #1 and Source #2. Then compare and contrast the way the author develops the central idea in each of the sources.

ABOUT THE AUTHOR

Nancy Boyles, Ed.D., was a classroom teacher for many years, and is now Professor Emerita at Southern Connecticut State University, where she was Professor of Reading and Graduate Reading Program Coordinator. She currently consults with districts and other organizations and agencies, providing both on-site and virtual workshops, modeling best practices in classrooms, and assisting with curriculum development. Nancy has written 12 books related to comprehension, a program for small group close reading instruction, and resources that integrate literacy and social emotional learning (SEL). Her SEL book, *Classroom Reading to Engage the Heart and Mind*, and two Quick Reference Guides, *Take Heart: Five SEL Mini-Units for Tough Times*, were published by W. W. Norton in 2020. Nancy lives in Truro, Massachusetts.